"Turning a complex situation into a simple story requires real effort. Tim Calkins makes getting there easy with a playbook that should be in the hands of any successful business leader today. Tim takes the guesswork out of business presentations with simple, no-nonsense tips that will pack punch, infuse energy and win audiences."

SALLY GRIMES, Group President, Tyson Foods

"Calkins reminds us that there is a process and structure for creating compelling presentations that will advance your ideas and your career. If your job involves selling or persuading, then you will benefit from applying the lessons of this book."

SERGIO PEREIRA, President, Quill.com

"Presenting is perhaps the single most important skill one can learn as an up-and-coming executive. Tim offers great, practical advice on how to radically improve."

TIM SIMONDS, President, Merrick Pet Care

"A smart, strategic and pragmatic approach for becoming a critical, confident and compelling presenter."

SCOTT M. DAVIS, Chief Growth Officer, Prophet

"Thoughtful guidance on how to master effective business presentations. I recommend this book for business professionals who seek to improve their effectiveness and grow their personal brand."

MARK JOHNSON, Vice President, Navistar Corporation

"Behind every big move in business is an idea that is well-communicated. Tim Calkins' book provides practical advice on how to prepare and deliver presentations that will make the difference when opportunity meets preparation. A must-read for first-time presenters and business pros."

CARRIE KURLANDER, Vice President, Public Relations, Chick-fil-A

"Tim Calkins brings to life the art and science of presenting and makes it easy to master one of the most challenging aspects in business. His approach allows professionals to gain alignment and move recommendations forward."

CARL GERLACH, President and Chief Executive Officer, Maple Hill Creamery

"Tim Calkins is known at Kellogg School of Management as one of the best presenters and storytellers. In this new book, he shares some of his secrets on how to make your presentation more effective. His tips are simple, easy to remember and valuable even if you consider yourself a master of presentations."

MIGUEL PATRICIO, Global CMO, Anheuser-Busch InBev

"Few individuals can capture an audience like Professor Calkins, and reading through these pages is like being in one of his dynamic and inspiring classes at Kellogg. This book is a powerful tool that will help you prepare and deliver epic presentations, both personal and professional."

LAWRENCE KIM, Vice President, Growth Officer, Taco Bell

"As Tim so convincingly demonstrates, relevant and engaging presentations are the perfect balance of 'what we say' and 'how we say it.' By following Tim's pragmatic approach, all of us will be better equipped to 'make the sale.'"

RICHARD H. LENNY, Non-Executive Chairman, Information Resources, Inc., former chairman and CEO, The Hershey Company

"Business leaders have to present well if they are going to have an impact. This book is the best one I've seen on creating and delivering an effective business presentation."

JOHN ANTON, CEO, Badger Sportswear

"My life would have been so much easier if presenters would have practiced what Professor Calkins is preaching in this book. A joy to read and stacked with clear takeaways. You will not regret reading this book—and your business presentations will be so much better."

BJÖRGVIN INGI ÓLAFSSON, Managing Partner, Deloitte Consulting Iceland

"During my twenty-seven years in consulting, I have delivered over 2,000 presentations. I wish somebody would have handed me a copy of this book on my first day on the job! I have now made it required reading for all of our consultants and handed a copy to many of my clients."

FERNANDO ASSENS, Founder and CEO, Argo Consulting

"Tim Calkins has absolutely nailed what it takes to deliver fantastic presentations."

CRAIG WORTMANN, CEO, Sales Engine, Inc.; Clinical Professor of Innovation and Entrepreneurship, Kellogg School of Management, Northwestern University

"This book is a must-read for anyone in a corporate or academic setting. If you aren't a highly confident presenter (and, let's be honest, who of us really is?) then you will become an increasingly confident presenter, and increasingly successful in your career after each short chapter."

STUART BAUM, President and Founder, LargerPond Marketing

"In the business world, how you show up in front of senior leaders is often more important to your career than *what* you accomplish 'behind the scenes.' This book does a great job boiling successful presentations down to some simple yet critical steps."

ERIC EPSTEIN, Marketing Director, Mars Wrigley Confectionery

"Tim offers practical advice, wrapped in compelling storytelling that makes this book a fun read. I will recommend it to both my clients and my colleagues."

JEFF GOURDJI, Partner, Healthcare Practice Leader, Prophet

"It is clear from reading Tim's book that everyone can become a great presenter. Great presenters are not born, they are made through hard work and practice! Applying the lessons in Tim's book guarantees your presentation skills will soar and your message will hit the bull's-eye."

DAN JAFFEE, President and CEO, Oil-Dri Corporation

HOW TO WASH A CHICKEN

Mastering the Business Presentation

Tim Calkins
KELLOGG SCHOOL OF MANAGEMENT

HOW TO
WASH A
CHICKEN

PAGE TWO
BOOKS

Cataloguing data available from Library and Archives Canada
ISBN 978-1-989025-03-1 (hardcover)
ISBN 978-1-989025-22-2 (ebook)

Produced by Page Two Books
www.pagetwobooks.com
Cover design by Peter Cocking
Cover photo courtesy iStockphoto
Interior design by Taysia Louie
Interior illustrations by Prateeba Perumal and Taysia Louie
Printed and bound in Canada by Friesens
Distributed in Canada by Raincoast Books
Distributed in the US and internationally by Publishers Group West
www.timcalkins.com

PREVIOUS TITLES

Breakthrough Marketing Plans: How to Stop Wasting Time and Start Driving Growth

Defending Your Brand: How Smart Companies Use Defensive Strategy to Deal with Competitive Attacks

Kellogg on Branding

CONTENTS

1

HOW TO WASH
A CHICKEN

"WASHING A CHICKEN is not a difficult task," I said to the audience. "Anyone can do it. If you are taking your bird to a poultry show, you really should give it a bath ahead of time to ensure the chicken looks its best. You just have to remember to keep the bird under control, use a gentle soap and dry the chicken thoroughly so it doesn't catch a cold." It was a cool day in March 1973. I was eight years old and giving my first official presentation at a competition sponsored by 4-H, an organization for young people.

A team of judges listened closely; this group evaluated each presentation, considering things like structure and delivery. At the end of the day, the judges gave each participant a score and some feedback. What went well? What could have been stronger? The panel awarded a blue ribbon to the best presentations, a red ribbon to the average ones and a white ribbon to the weaker presentations.

Pointing to my poster, I then described the process for washing a chicken in detail. After walking the audience through the steps,

I bent down and pulled out a large plastic crate from behind the desk at the front of the room.

"Now, let me demonstrate precisely how to do it," I continued. I opened up the crate and reached in. The energetic White Leghorn chicken ran to the far end of the box, just out of my reach. I stuck my head and shoulders into the crate and reached out my hand; I could just touch the bird. Concerned, the hen started running back and forth along the back wall of the crate, clearly upset about the unfolding events.

If you've ever raised chickens, you know that there is a right way and a wrong way to pick up a bird. The right way is to put your hands over the chicken's wings and gently lift it up in the air. The chicken will quickly realize that it can't flap its wings, and after a few minutes it will stop struggling and settle down. You can then turn the bird around to inspect it. Or, as in my case, you can give it a bath.

The wrong way to pick up a chicken is any other method. If you grab hold of a foot, the tail or even just one wing, the situation will quickly deteriorate. You have to have control of the wings, because the chicken—naturally concerned about its safety—will flap them wildly in a bid to escape. White Leghorns, the breed I was working with that day, are particularly nervous and flighty creatures.

As I reached into the crate, I was a bit anxious about my presentation and eager to keep everything moving along. Each presenter had only a few minutes, and the judges kept close track of the time. So I reached for the chicken and grabbed hold of the white tail and just pulled the bird out of the crate. And the chaos began.

THE LEGHORN, CERTAIN it was soon to meet its demise as a prop in a presentation on processing a chicken, flapped it wings, batting me in the face and chest. Dust and dirt flew while white feathers filled the room. I held on to the tail with one hand, trying to keep a chicken from getting loose in the middle of my first presentation. My audience, excited to see precisely how this lively scene would turn out, leaned forward. I did my best to calmly continue with my presentation while dealing with the frantic hen.

"Keeping the chicken under control is really very important. Otherwise it will panic and flap, like this hen is doing," I observed, as feathers snowed down and the hen cried out in distress. "Sometimes it takes a little while to get the hen settled."

The battle went on for what seemed—to me—like hours. It was excruciating. Eventually the chicken grew tired, so I was able to slip my arm over its wings and trap it next to my body.

Relieved, I continued. "Once you have the chicken under control, you simply place it in the sink," I explained as I put the (now) subdued chicken in the bucket of warm soapy water in front of me. "Remember to use a very gentle soap."

I reached for the soap, and the chicken, sensing its opportunity, rallied and tried again to escape. One wing slipped from my grasp. More flapping ensued: another great struggle. Only this time water was flying around, too. I was drenched.

Eventually I regained control of the situation, completed the washing and dried the bird using my mother's hair dryer. "It is important to dry the chicken thoroughly, but be careful when using a dryer," I cautioned. "It can be too hot. Medium heat works best." Then, keeping my hands firmly on the wings, I put the hen back in the crate.

"And that is how you wash a chicken," I summarized. "Remember the three keys to success: keep control of the bird, use a gentle detergent and dry it thoroughly. It is really a very easy process."

I was exhausted, wet and covered in feathers. But I was done and thrilled to put the presentation behind me. People clapped enthusiastically as I picked up my things; it was surely one of the most exciting presentations of the day. I took my seat to watch the next presentation.

Later that afternoon when the judges handed out the awards, I found myself with a prized blue ribbon and a top score. In their

comments, the judges raved about my presentation. They especially loved the demonstration with the chicken.

I learned three important things that day.

First, presenting is a thrill. It is scary, exciting and energizing
all at the same time. You are the center of attention.

Second, it helps if you follow some simple rules. Things like
an introduction, a conclusion, a clear story and simple visual aids
really help. The basics are not too complicated.

Third, a good presentation can make anything interesting
and engaging, and if you want to capture people's attention, it is
always good to have some dynamic props. A flapping, squawking
chicken works pretty well. It certainly wakes people up.

Five Thousand Presentations

Since that day, I have delivered more than five thousand presentations.[1] In some ways, my early experience with that hen set the
course for my career.

In middle school and high school, I did a number of those 4-H
presentations. I talked about raising pigs, breeding ducks and col-
lecting butterflies. I never tackled the chicken-washing topic again.

After college, I spent two years in management consulting
with the strategy firm Booz Allen, where I spent much of my time
creating and delivering project presentations for clients in the
insurance, energy and consumer packaged goods industries.

I then went to Harvard Business School for my MBA, and I
later took a job at Kraft Foods working in brand management. I
managed a series of different businesses during my eleven years
at Kraft, including Parkay Margarine, A.1. Steak Sauce, Miracle
Whip, Taco Bell and Kraft BBQ Sauce. In each of the roles, I spent
my time developing and presenting business updates, project recommendations and marketing plans.

After five years at Kraft, I began teaching a course in advertising at DeVry University's business school as an adjunct professor. Later I moved to Northwestern University's Kellogg School of Management. Eventually, I realized I enjoyed teaching more than the day-to-day struggle of shipping trucks of Kraft BBQ Sauce, so when I had the chance to become a clinical professor—which meant I would receive an office and a salary—I left Kraft and made Kellogg my primary base.

I now spend my time helping people build strong businesses and great brands. I teach a number of courses at Kellogg in the full-time, part-time and executive MBA programs, including Marketing Strategy, Strategic Marketing Decisions and Biomedical Marketing. I also lead seminars for companies all over the world. In recent years, I've worked with firms such as Eli Lilly, Novartis, AbbVie, IIP, Hyatt, PwC and Textron. This has taken me to countries including Russia, Australia, Japan, Denmark, Dubai, Jordan, Germany, Switzerland, China and Turkey.

Along the way, I picked up some teaching prizes. I won the Sidney J. Levy Teaching Award, two Kellogg Faculty Impact Awards, and four Kellogg Executive MBA Top Professor Awards. I also received Kellogg's top teaching prize, the L.G. Lavengood Outstanding Professor of the Year Award, in two different years, making me one of just five people to have won it twice in the award's more than forty year history. The MBA website *Poets & Quants* included me on its list of "Favorite MBA Professors of 2016."

All of this has given me an appreciation for the power of a good presentation. I know just how impactful a strong update can be; it can sway a group, gain agreement, secure approval and motivate a team.

You can have the best idea in the world, but it will only catch on if you can present it well. In some respects, taking a recommendation to business leaders is like taking a chicken to a poultry show. You want to clean it up so that it looks its best.

2

ABOUT THIS BOOK

THIS BOOK HAS one simple goal: to help you create and deliver an effective business presentation. If you read this book—and apply the lessons—you will present with more confidence and conviction. You will be smoother in front of a group and more in control of the room.

Becoming a better speaker will lead to other, more important benefits. If you improve your presenting skills, you will almost certainly be more successful in your job. People will be more likely to approve your recommendations, which will help you have a bigger impact on the business. When your work becomes more impactful, senior management will think more highly of you. Your personal brand will strengthen.

When you're more successful in your job, you will receive a bigger bonus. You'll get a raise and eventually a promotion. The move up the ranks will lead to a higher salary and an even bigger bonus, along with some stock options. Eventually you will have larger and more exciting opportunities that give you a chance to have an even more significant impact on the business.

All this progress will give you a sense of purpose and direction in your life. Ultimately, it will make you more successful, more prosperous and more confident.

In short, this book—by helping you become a better presenter—will improve your life.

The Problem

"Good evening!" I welcomed my class of MBA students at DeVry University's business school. It was a cold November evening. "Tonight we have team presentations," I continued. "We have a lot to get to, so we should dive right in. Let me introduce our first group. Here is team number one. Take it away, team number one!"

The group of students slowly and hesitantly came to the front of the room. They gathered around the podium and fumbled with the cables to connect the computer to the projection system. The team spent about five minutes trying different connections and talking about potential issues while their classmates and I watched.

Eventually, the first slide filled the screen. One of the students centered himself behind the podium, looked down at the computer and read the title of the presentation out loud. He then clicked to the next slide, which was a page full of numbers.

"Here is the market share analysis by quarter and by region," he said. He focused intently on his computer.

"You can see that the share is 34 percent. In our most important segment, it is 26 percent," he continued. The student nodded his head and moved on to another page, this one showing a detailed SWOT analysis: strengths, weaknesses, opportunities and threats.

"The business has a number of strengths and weaknesses," he explained. "There are also opportunities and threats. The main opportunity is the size of the market. The biggest threat is competition."

He moved on to the next page, and students in the class shifted in their seats, clearly bored. The presenter clicked to a slide titled "Competitive Analysis." Still looking down, he continued speaking. "There are four large competitors, as you can see here. All of them have several different brands."

He pressed on through more slides, reviewing pages titled "Customer Segmentation," "Pricing Trends" and "Financials."

It didn't take long for him to lose the audience entirely. I looked around the room and noted the scene. Some of the students were staring off into space, presumably thinking about their plans for the break or the attractive student they'd bumped into at the gym that morning. Others were studying their own slides, preparing for their presentations. A few students were subtly checking emails. One fellow was asleep in the second row.

It was a painful experience for the presenter and for the viewers.

Unfortunately, this situation is all too common; many people simply don't present well. The slides are cluttered, there is no story or clear recommendation, the delivery is dull.

This is a huge problem. The best recommendation in the world will seem feeble if presented in a sloppy manner; the smartest business executive will seem ineffective and weak.

Poor presentations like this aren't usually due to a lack of effort. In most cases, the presenters are really trying to do well. The students I teach, for example, are smart and motivated. They invest significant time and money to go to business school. They have high expectations for themselves, their classmates and their professors—so they work hard. When creating a presentation, they consider the flow and the data, think about the recommendation and support their points. Despite all this work, though, the effort often falls flat, because the reality is that all too many people just don't know how to create and deliver an effective presentation.

Everyone Can Present Well

I believe that everyone can give an effective presentation.
There isn't anything secret about presenting. The necessary skills are simple, the keys to success are clear, and the problems are easy to identify and correct.

You don't need to be trained in theater to present well. You don't need to have the humor of Jerry Seinfeld or the looks of Brad Pitt or the stage presence of Taylor Swift. You simply need to think logically, prepare diligently and speak clearly. It doesn't require special skills or gifts. Chris Anderson is head of TED, perhaps the most famous platform for public speaking today. He observes, "Facility with public speaking is not a gift granted at birth to the lucky few. It's a broad-ranging set of skills." [1]

Many people point to British prime minister Winston Churchill as one of the great orators of the twentieth century. His speeches motivated and inspired, creating feelings of confidence and commitment. Yet Churchill was not born with a gift for public speaking. On the contrary, he stammered and had a lisp. He became a great speaker because he knew it was important for his career, and he worked hard to improve his skills.

Anyone who sets their mind to it can become a strong presenter. By employing some commonsense techniques, even the most socially awkward person can deliver a presentation that is effective and clear. It might not bring people to tears or inspire a standing ovation, but it will accomplish the task.

Everyone Can Present Better

Everyone can present well, and everyone can present better. Presenting isn't a skill you master and then declare it done; it is a constant challenge. There is always room for improvement.

In this way, presenting is different than riding a bicycle. When learning how to master a bike, you practice and practice. Someone gives you a hand and steadies you. Your parent might guide you along as the bike starts to gain momentum. Eventually you figure it out; you learn how to accelerate, gain speed and stop. And once you have the skill, you tend to keep it. People don't forget how to ride a bike. They don't say, "Well, Joe, I haven't ridden a bike in a couple years. Do you think you could steady me for a while?" They just remember.

Presenting is different.

Presenting is a set of skills and techniques that one can learn. Still, every presentation could be better. Perhaps the introduction could be tighter, or the support could be stronger. You might have rushed the first section or run out of time, and, of course, it is hard to catch every typo. Maybe you stumbled when responding to a question.

This means that there is always a chance to improve. Every presentation is an opportunity to communicate more effectively. Even the best presenter can find ways to perform just a little bit better.

Room for Improvement

In an effort to understand how people view presenting, I recently completed several surveys with my MBA students at Northwestern University's Kellogg School of Management. In total, I received responses from 379 people.

I asked a variety of questions, including the following:

- Do you enjoy presenting?
- Do you get nervous when presenting?
- How good are you at creating and delivering presentations?
- How easy is it for you to construct a presentation?
- How much training have you received on presenting?

The results were remarkable and not particularly encouraging. The first takeaway: people don't like presenting. The average response to the question "Do you enjoy presenting?" on a scale of 1 to 10 was just 7.0 on one survey and 6.5 on another.

People also don't think they are very good at presenting. On the question of "How good are you at creating and delivering presentations?" the average scores were 6.8 and 6.6 out of 10. These are not impressive figures, especially when you remember that people tend to be optimistic—studies consistently show that on topics such as intelligence and appearance, the vast majority of people think they are well above average.

Students don't think their classmates are very effective, either. When I asked them how effective their classmates were at creating and delivering presentations, the average score was just 6.8 out of 10.

So here is the unfortunate situation: people don't enjoy presenting, don't think they are particularly good at it and don't think their peers are good at it, either. This is a problem.

Three Segments

One striking thing that emerged from my research was that people have very different feelings about presenting. Behind the averages are distinct groups.

I WAS ABLE to identify three segments. The first group I call the Confident Presenters. This group makes up about 30 percent of students. These people enjoy presenting, think they are good at it and find it relatively easy.

On the other extreme is a group best named the Struggling Presenters. These people have a very different view of things. They don't enjoy presenting, don't think they are very good at it, find it difficult and get very nervous. This group is about 25 percent of students.

In the middle are the Solid Presenters, about 45 percent of people.

I saw the groups emerge in multiple surveys. Below are highlights from two.

Exhibit 1-1 Views of Presenting FALL 2017 SURVEY	Confident Presenters	Solid Presenters	Struggling Presenters
Percentage of Respondents	30.4%	43.5%	26.1%
How good are you at presenting? (1 is poor, 10 is excellent)	8.0	6.6	4.6
How easy is it for you? (1 is very difficult, 10 is very easy)	7.1	6.3	4.9
Do you get nervous when presenting? (1 is not nervous, 10 is very nervous)	4.6	5.5	5.8

Exhibit 1-2 Views of Presenting WINTER 2017 SURVEY	Confident Presenters	Solid Presenters	Struggling Presenters
Percentage of Respondents	25.5%	45.1%	29.4%
Compared to others, how good are you? (1 is worse, 10 is much better)	8.0	6.8	4.8
How easy is it for you? (1 is very difficult, 10 is very easy)	7.9	6.5	4.1
Do you get nervous when presenting? (1 is not nervous, 10 is very nervous)	3.5	5.3	7.5

Reinforcing Cycles

Presenting can quickly become reinforcing. People who are good presenters will likely get even better over time, while people who are weak presenters will get worse.

This happens for three reasons. First, people who fall in the Confident Presenters segment will get more practice. When there is an opportunity to deliver an update, they raise their hands and volunteer. After all, they are pretty good at it and generally enjoy it.

People in the Struggling Presenters group will naturally try to avoid presentations, since they find the experience to be difficult and scary. They look for any possible reason not to present.

The impact is that people who think they are better at presenting will get more practice, which will then make them still better at presenting. People who don't like to present won't get much practice and won't improve.

The second dynamic is that people who like presenting will spend more time preparing. They will dive right into the project and get started. It is, after all, an exciting and largely positive time.

People who don't like to present will probably procrastinate. Who wants to even think about a presentation when it will be scary and probably won't go well?

The result is that the people in the Confident Presenters group will have more time to perfect the presentation, making refinements to the argument and polishing the slides; those in the Struggling Presenters segment will scramble to get ready.

Finally, people who are Confident Presenters will be more assured. They think they are good presenters, so they are less nervous. They speak loudly and step forward in a confident manner.

Struggling Presenters will have a different experience. Because they are nervous, they might rush or stumble over words. They may read the slides or focus on their computer. They will avoid making eye contact with the audience.

ABOUT THIS BOOK   15

Combined, all of these factors mean that Confident Present-ers, with practice and positive outcomes, will tend to improve over time. The Struggling Presenters will continue to struggle. The Solid Presenters will remain average.

The Circle of Presenting Success will propel Confident Present-ers forward, and the Circle of Presenting Doom will pull down Struggling Presenters.

Exhibit 1-3 Circle of Presenting Success

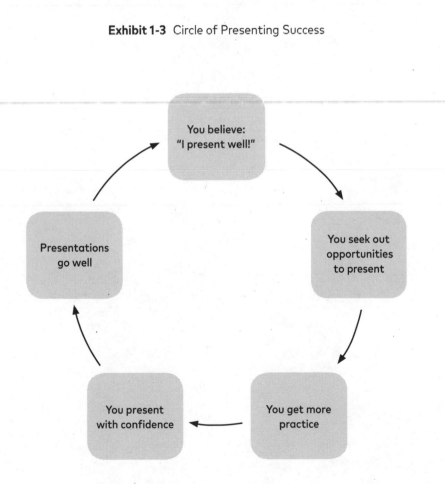

Exhibit 1-4 Circle of Presenting Doom

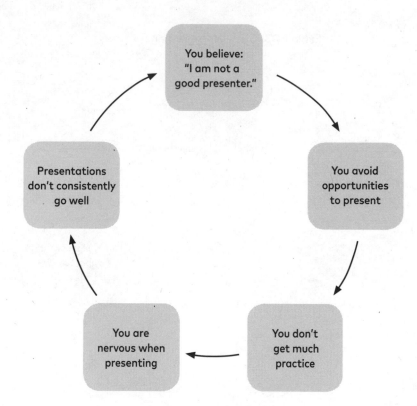

A Lack of Training

In my student surveys I asked about training. Most people replied that they had received some training in presenting skills, but not much. Across my different surveys, the average response to the question "How much training have you received on presenting?" was just 5.8 (1 was nothing, 10 was a lot).

Training varied between the segments. In every survey, people in the Confident Presenters group reported that they had received much more training than those in the Struggling Presenters segment.

Exhibit 1-5 Views of Training:
How Much Training Have You Received?

FALL 2015 SURVEY

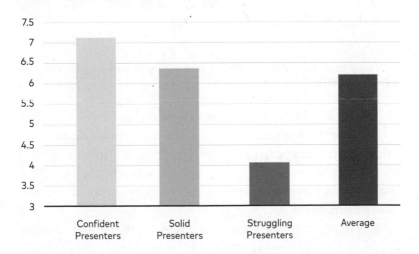

From this data, one might conclude that training is essential for developing presentation skills. Clearly, the Confident Presenters benefited from all the training and the Struggling Presenters didn't.

I suspect the story isn't quite this simple because the causality isn't clear. Did training drive this difference? Perhaps. But it might just be that people who like presenting and think they are good at it tend to sign up for presentation training programs. People who *don't* like presenting *don't* seek out the programs.

I notice this dynamic with my colleagues at Kellogg. When there is a seminar on teaching techniques, perhaps a review of ways to establish positive classroom norms or a discussion about fostering debate, the best teachers show up. Professor David Besanko, for example, might be the top teacher at Kellogg; he is the only person to have won the L.G. Lavengood Award, the top teaching prize, three times. Considering that you're only eligible to win this award once every five years, that is quite an accomplishment. Whenever there is a seminar on teaching, David shows up. He clearly doesn't need the help. I suspect he just loves thinking and learning about teaching.

Still, training is an important way to improve your presenting skills. How else will someone improve?

The Bottom Line

This book will help you deliver better presentations whether you're a new college graduate or an established professional. You can find something useful in here if you're working for a not-for-profit organization, a corporation or a government agency. The characteristics of a great presentation don't really change from one industry to the next.

People who are Confident Presenters will find this book to be a refresher; it will provide some validation. Many of the concepts and ideas will resonate; I suspect you are using many of these already. This is a chance to compare what you are doing with these best practices and find opportunities to improve even more.

Solid Presenters can use this book to get to the next level. It will reinforce some of your practices and provide concrete suggestions to propel you forward to the Confident Presenters segment.

Those in the Struggling Presenters group will benefit from the tips and suggestions. Consistently using these practical ideas and approaches will improve your overall presenting skills. If you have a bit of success, you might be inclined to present more often. This can lead to additional success. It can start you on the Circle of Presenting Success, where one good presentation leads to another. Experience leads to confidence, and confidence contributes to success.

This is not a general book about public speaking. I don't discuss poetry slams, karaoke or cowboy storytelling contests. I don't spend time on debate strategy or how to give a toast at a wedding.

It is a guide for business leaders and, in particular, people on their way up.

3

PICK YOUR MOMENT

THE FIRST STEP in developing a great presentation is simple: ask yourself if you really have to do the presentation at all. If there isn't a compelling need, you should save yourself and your audience a lot of time and just skip it.

Great presenters know when they need to present and when they don't. Picking the right moment to present is an important part of the process, and you want to set yourself up for success.

Don't Waste People's Time

Many people (most people?) hate attending meetings and sitting through presentations. They lampoon these events as a grand waste of time. PowerPoint takes much of the blame; people are quick to attack it as an evil program that consumes time and dulls the mind. People joke about Death by PowerPoint.

In many cases, however, the problem isn't the presenter or the software platform. It is a more basic issue: there was no need for the presentation at all. A simple way to put someone to sleep is to show them a lot of information that isn't particularly important or relevant.

The point is simple. If you don't need to do a presentation on a particular topic, if there isn't a compelling reason—don't. As Sun Tzu, the great military strategist, supposedly said, "The greatest victory is that which requires no battle." [1] The same could be said for presentations. The best presentation may well be the one you decide to not give at all.

There are several benefits to not presenting. One compelling reason to skip the presentation is that you'll save yourself a lot of time. A theme that carries through this book is that creating a great presentation isn't easy. It takes time and effort. You have to craft the story, find key pieces of data, refine the pages, polish the document, presell the material, practice and set the stage. It isn't simple, and it isn't quick.

If you don't present, you save all the time and energy you otherwise would have spent. You can devote this to actually making progress on your projects and having an impact on the business. Or you can just leave work early and spend time with your family.

Another reason to avoid a presentation is to enhance your reputation. A weak business update can damage your personal brand; it may make people think you don't have a good grasp of the business. People are rarely enchanted by an irrelevant presentation; delivering one doesn't make you look good.

There is a very real chance that an interesting but not essential presentation will go poorly. Your audience is busy. If you ask them to sit through a lot of information that isn't directly relevant to them, they will probably be impatient. They may be grumpy. They might interrupt with difficult questions or just tune out and check emails. All of this makes it difficult for you to deliver a good presentation. It is hard to capture energy and positive spirits when your audience isn't engaged.

By presenting only when you need to, you make your presentations more important. This in turn makes you look better; whenever people see you presenting, you are covering notable material, and your audience is engaged and interested.

In short, if you can avoid a presentation, do it.

When to Present

There are times when you need to do a presentation and times when you don't. Understanding the difference is critical. You want to present with vigor and energy when it is necessary, and avoiding unnecessary presentations is one way to make sure you do that.

Here are several occasions that often call for a presentation.

YOU NEED PEOPLE TO MAKE A DECISION

It can be difficult to get people to agree to a recommendation. You send an email to the key people and get no reply. You send a follow-up email and still—silence. Eventually someone replies to the entire group, requesting a few small changes. Someone else bounces back with a question, which you answer. Based on the input, you update the document and send it around again. Someone else then asks for a few changes to this new version, while someone else replies to the original email and asks the same question that someone else asked earlier. You prepare another update, which leads to more requests for changes. The situation can go on and on. The reality is that many people don't like to make decisions. Thinking about a topic is fine. Deciding? Not so much. Deciding takes work and energy. There is commitment and risk involved. It is easier to just delay.

You can certainly see this when it comes to vacations. Many people enjoy thinking about a vacation. You might ponder the various options. You wonder, "Perhaps we should go to Spain this year. Of course, France is lovely. And I've always wanted to take the kids to Japan; that is truly a remarkable country. Japan is safe, too. Still, Iceland seems hot right now, what with the new nonstop flights..." Actually choosing where to go is much more difficult. If you settle on Spain, then you aren't going to France or Japan. Who wants to turn down France and Japan? It is much easier to debate a little longer, keeping all the options in the mix.

The same is true when it comes to strategic business decisions. Should we launch the new product this year or not? There are certainly some compelling reasons to move forward. It might be a huge success. At the same time, there is a lot of risk. It really isn't clear what will happen. It is very easy to just push the decision off for a couple weeks.

One of the most effective ways to force a decision is to get the key people together in a room and discuss it. You present the issue and the different points of view with a presentation, lay out the recommendation and then you say to the group, "We really need to make a decision on this today. The time is now." The group then can review, discuss and debate. Even if you don't finalize the decision, you can encourage people to identify the main issues. What evidence do we need to be comfortable with the decision? What do we have to study to make the final call?

YOU NEED SUPPORT

Getting support is critical in any organization. If you don't have people behind you, an initiative can stumble. People might second-guess things. Resources may not appear. The program might not happen at all. More likely it might remain far down the priority list, making limited headway.

This is certainly true when it comes to cross-functional colleagues. It is all too easy for your head of sales to cautiously endorse a particular program. This isn't going to help; you need real support. Your finance counterpart may indicate that the proposition looks okay but then raise all sorts of challenging questions at the last minute.

You also need support from senior management. If the vice president or CEO believes in a project, they will make it a priority. They will give it attention and—more important—money.

If you don't have senior management support, you have a major task ahead. Perhaps an impossible task. How do you get a major project successfully out the door without support from the top people? You don't.

For several reasons, a presentation can be a highly effective way to get people on board and generate enthusiasm. One reason is that a presentation gives you a chance to take people through your logic and rationale. You can clearly state, "I think this is a good move for the company, and here is why it should work." When you are presenting, you have everyone's focus and attention. This is a gift. You can make your case and sell the recommendation.

Another reason is that a presentation can force public commitment. If you can get the head of sales to say, "I think this is a terrific idea," then you have them on board. It is very difficult for them to then back away. The result is that a public commitment leads to longer-term support. The head of sales isn't likely to come back later and point out deep concerns about the project. And if they are worried, their focus will be on finding a solution, not just identifying problems.

When you ask for help, one of two things will occur. Both are good. One possibility is that you will get assistance; senior executives will see the issue and understand the need. They will provide extra resources that will help you address the problems. The other possibility is that you won't get support; senior management tells you to do the best you can. This isn't actually a terrible outcome, though. You saw the issue, asked for help, then senior management decided to not provide the assistance—in some ways, you are now off the hook.

I saw this dynamic when I was managing the Shake 'n Bake brand, a line of chicken-seasoning products. At the time, sales were dropping at an alarming pace; it was quite clear that we were not on track to make our annual financial objectives. I put together a business update with my team, in which we analyzed the drivers of the situation and recommended a plan to address them. The plan was expensive, however. The brand needed new advertising, new packaging and a major in-store promotion effort.

Ultimately, the division head elected to not proceed with the investment; resources were limited and there were other brands having more significant issues.

It wasn't the outcome I was hoping for, but I knew that my team came across as proactive, competent and energetic. If the business continued to slide, we were safe; we had developed a plan to fix things. We just were not able to implement the bulk of it due to other priorities in the division.

YOU NEED PEOPLE TO UNDERSTAND A SITUATION

There are times when you need to tell people about the business, when you need to bring them up to speed. A presentation can be an effective way to do this, because you have the opportunity to review the information and explain it. Sending the information in an email is another option, but people often don't read emails. Texts command more attention but are not suitable for longer updates. Memos are even more difficult; people often work remotely, so physical pieces of paper may not get to them. If you need someone to really understand a situation, a meeting can be a powerful tool.

During my time at Kraft Foods, the firm acquired Nabisco, another large us-based food company. I was senior director of the Meat Enhancement Category at the time, a collection of businesses that included Kraft BBQ Sauce, Bull's-Eye BBQ Sauce, Shake 'n Bake, Oven Fry and other brands. Nabisco owned A.1. Steak Sauce, so this brand joined my portfolio after the acquisition.

It didn't take long for me to realize that there was a problem. Nabisco executives had launched a line of A.1. marinades several years earlier, and the A.1. business plan assumed that these items would grow in a dramatic fashion. Unfortunately, business trends suggested that these forecasts were not likely to materialize. Instead of growing at a robust pace, the marinade line was starting to stagnate. The initial sales bump reflected store stocking and initial customer trial driven by deep promotional price cuts. Repeat purchases were not coming in as anticipated, indicating there was a problem with the core product proposition. The slowing sales created a significant gap in the budget; the business would soon be short of its profit target by millions of dollars.

I wasn't entirely sure how to respond to the developing crisis; I was new to the A.1. business and didn't know all the available levers. But I knew that this was a major problem for Kraft; it isn't possible to close a multimillion-dollar gap in the budget on mature, well-established businesses like Kraft BBQ Sauce and A.1. Steak Sauce.

My first move was to schedule a business update with senior management. I needed the executive team leading Kraft to understand the financial risk. I would attempt to close the gap, of course, but it wasn't clear that I could. By highlighting the problem quickly, I would avoid giving the executives a notable and most unwelcome surprise at the end of the year. Causing the company to miss its financial targets is not a good way to build your personal brand and secure your spot on the fast track.

Sometimes informing people is a solid reason to hold a meeting. If you want to be sure that people hear your message, you need to get them in the room and sit them down. Only then can you be confident that they've heard your perspective and gotten your point.

YOUR BOSS WANTS YOU TO

If your boss says you should do a presentation, generally, you should do a presentation. In most organizations, you do what you are asked to do.

It is fair, of course, to question the decision and ask for a delay. Is this the right time? Is the recommendation tight enough at this point? Would an additional week or two of analysis result in a much stronger update? Ultimately, however, it is your boss's decision. If they want you to present, present.

This is true for two reasons. First, bosses matter. If they like you and support you, good things tend to happen. You will get a good bonus and raise. You might get a promotion. You could be included in some interesting, high-level discussions. Bosses don't want to hear why you won't do what they have asked you to do. They want to know how fast you will do it.

Second, your boss may understand certain organizational dynamics that you don't. It could be that there are other projects moving forward. You aren't aware of these, but your boss is. You might be up for a promotion and senior management wants another chance to evaluate your skills. Ultimately, you have to trust your boss to make good decisions based on an understanding of the broader organizational situation.

When You Shouldn't Present

The more appealing question: When should you cancel the presentation? When can you save the time? There are a number of situations when canceling will be your best move.

YOU CAN COMMUNICATE THE INFORMATION IN A DIFFERENT, MORE CONCISE WAY

Informing people about routine matters is not a compelling reason to present. You can just send information in an email. Remember, people read faster than they speak. If a memo, email, text or tweet will suffice, great.

THE RECOMMENDATION ISN'T CLEAR

You shouldn't present a recommendation until you are confident that you understand the situation and have a plan. The support should be logical. You should have thought through the different dynamics and considered the key questions.

If you haven't finished your analysis, you shouldn't present. Moving forward will simply highlight that you aren't prepared. You will be uncertain and nervous, and this will come across. People will ask questions, searching for the flaws in the analysis, and they will find them. It will not end well.

Presenting without a clear recommendation can also limit your options. A senior executive may be led to a conclusion based on a partial update. They might exclaim, "Wow! Look at that. This really is a pricing issue, isn't it? We have to realign pricing. How fast can we make the change?" You might be weeks away from finalizing your point of view, but the senior executive has already come to a conclusion. Getting someone to change their opinion is not an easy task.

THERE ARE VERY DIFFERENT POINTS OF VIEW

When you deliver a presentation, you hope that your audience will agree. Conflict is rarely the desired outcome; you don't want hostility, challenges and disputes. Discussion is good; disagreement is not.

If you know that your team doesn't agree on a particular topic, you shouldn't be presenting. You should spend the time instead working through the issues, understanding why people don't agree and searching for some common ground.

The Last-Minute Cancellation

Canceling a presentation is not ideal. Canceling a meeting at the last minute is particularly problematic; the move will not enhance your reputation. It suggests you are not prepared. It will raise doubts about your recommendation, and it will definitely make you look bad. It is hard to find glory with a last-minute cancellation.

Still, sometimes the right move, the best thing you can do, is to cancel at the last minute. There are several reasons why this might be the case.

THE PRESENTATION ISN'T READY

If you aren't done with the presentation, you shouldn't present it. Remember that there is a difference between being done and being perfect. You want your presentation to be good, but it doesn't have to be perfect. Remember the famous line: "Don't let perfect be the enemy of good."

It is almost impossible to make a presentation perfect. There are so many things to consider, refine and think about that trying to get the document perfect means that it will never be finished. Perfection isn't the goal.

At the same time, you shouldn't move ahead with a presentation that is clearly lacking. Poor formatting, typos, mistakes, improper sequencing and other problems create the wrong impression. It can be difficult to recover from these impressions. First impressions matter! Worst case, your strong analysis and recommendation will be questioned because of the weak presentation.

Before you get to a presentation, evaluate where you are. If it isn't close to done, you should seriously consider delaying for a couple days.

YOU AREN'T CONFIDENT IN THE ANALYSIS

One of the worst feelings is realizing that your analysis doesn't work shortly before you are supposed to present it. Perhaps you made a mistake in the regression analysis. Maybe a cell in the spreadsheet linked to a cell it wasn't supposed to. For one reason or another, the analysis isn't correct. There are two problems with presenting a troubled analysis. The first is that you will not be confident in the data, and that will come through in the presentation. If you know the numbers are wrong, you won't stand up straight, look people in the eye and speak with a confident voice.

The second problem is that your audience might uncover the error. It isn't easy to find the flaw in an analysis from a presentation, especially if the presenter is moving right along from slide to slide. So you will probably be fine. But sometimes you won't.

The issue is that some people are smart and have an inherent feel for the business. In this case, a number that is a bit off might stand out. That will lead to a question. And this will lead to another question.

Eventually, you will probably be forced to punt, stating, "Well, I will look at that part of the analysis again," or "I would be happy to meet with you to take you through the analysis."

This is a painful situation. You know your credibility has been knocked down. Your audience knows this, too.

If you learn that there is a mistake in your analysis, you should not present it. You should drop the page or the section if you can. Sometimes this will mean that the presentation itself won't work. In that case, you should postpone the discussion until another day when the numbers are right.

It is better to ask to reschedule than to damage your reputation for accuracy. Once people lose faith in your ability to do the numbers, they will question everything you do.

YOUR AUDIENCE IS DISTRACTED BY ANOTHER CRISIS

On September 11, 2001, I was scheduled to present an update on the Kraft BBQ Sauce business to Betsy Holden, then-CEO of Kraft Foods. It was an important meeting for me. I had been running the business for several years, but the financial results were disappointing because it was taking time for the turnaround plan to kick in. My career was at stake. If the meeting went well, I could continue to manage the business and perhaps find myself in line for a promotion. If it went poorly, I would be asked to start thinking about my other interests. People were rarely fired at Kraft; managers just encouraged people to think about alternatives and the best path. A severance plan provided a bit more encouragement.

I was ready for the presentation. I had spent several weeks developing the deck. I worked on the flow and developed headlines that told a story. Each page had the right amount of information—not too much and not too little. My team had worked hard checking each data point and financial figure. We were ready to roll.

The meeting was set for 2 p.m.

That morning an airplane crashed into one of the World Trade Center towers in New York. Then another plane crashed into the second tower. The country was under attack.

I immediately called off the meeting, despite the fact that rescheduling would be difficult and likely require a new round of revisions to reflect the latest data.

The thing is, you don't want to proceed with a meeting when you know your key audience is focused on other things. It is better to delay, find a time when you can get solid focus, and reschedule.

If you proceed, your audience simply won't be listening. They might frequently check their mobile device or even get up and walk out in the middle of the meeting. This is an easy way to destroy the momentum of a presentation. They won't be focused on you, so all of your thinking and effort will be a waste.

You will never get perfect attention, of course. There is simply too much happening in the world, and senior executives have a lot on their plates. They will always have *something* on their mind. A bit of distraction doesn't matter; you can rise above that and capture their attention with a lively presentation. When your audience is *very* focused on something else, however, it is best to step back and find a new time.

YOU DON'T HAVE CROSS-FUNCTIONAL SUPPORT

It is hard to present without support. If you learn that some of your colleagues oppose your recommendation, you usually should delay the presentation to another day. There is nothing worse than being in the middle of a presentation when someone from your team wavers in their support.

Senior executives want to be confident that things will go well. They are often nervous about being on the receiving end of a half-baked recommendation for a project that will ultimately go poorly and damage their reputation. One way they become confident is by seeing a team with conviction. If everyone agrees with a plan, then it certainly is a more compelling recommendation. If the head of sales, the head of operations, the head of finance and the head of market research all say that it makes sense, then it is hard for a senior executive to stop it.

Executives become nervous when there isn't agreement. It is a bad sign when the head of sales shifts in her seat and looks down. Picking up on this, the senior executive might then fire off a question: "So, Susan, are you on board with this recommendation?"

You want Susan to lean forward and reply, "That is absolutely right. I've been through this entire plan, and it all works well. Just two days ago, I was down in Memphis and ran this by the region head. She agreed it all looks good."

If Susan hesitates, there is a problem. She might state, "I certainly see the logic behind the recommendation, but I am not confident the sales team can execute this plan." Or she might comment, "I just don't think this is going to be successful."

Once Susan wavers, the entire presentation loses credibility. Why would the senior executive support this? There are clearly issues. The only possible resolution is that the top person will ask to revisit the recommendation in a few weeks. This is not a positive outcome.

So if you learn that you have issues on your team, it may make sense to delay the presentation. You need to figure out where people are before moving forward.

Now, everyone may not agree with every presentation. This is life. People can have different points of view. But you need to know where you stand before the presentation so that it reflects the situation. If you have different opinions on the team, you can do some pre-work to gain alignment. Or you can create a presentation where you introduce two different options, present-ing the pros and cons of each.

If you learn at the last minute that you don't have team agree-ment, then delaying the meeting is the best course. There is no reason to go into a meeting when you know your team has signifi-cant concerns. In this situation you are not set up for success, and the meeting probably won't go too well.

4

BE CLEAR ON
THE PURPOSE

ONCE YOU'VE DECIDED to present, you need to sit back and clarify the purpose. Why exactly are you presenting? What do you hope to achieve? If you are not clear on the purpose, the presentation is not likely to go well.

The Importance of Clarity

There is a famous scene in *Alice in Wonderland* where Alice is talking with the Cheshire Cat.

> "Would you tell me, please, which way I ought to go from here?"
> "That depends a good deal on where you want to get to," said the Cat.
> "I don't much care where—," said Alice.
> "Then it doesn't matter which way you go," said the Cat.[1]

It is an insightful observation by the Cheshire Cat. Without a sense of the goal, you are lost. Any direction might be right *or* wrong. You need to know your destination before you get too far into a journey, or you won't know which way to go. Are you trying to get to Miami or Tokyo?

This is certainly the case with a presentation. You can't make any meaningful progress until you know your objective. As presenting consultant Jerry Weissman writes, "The only sure way to create a successful presentation is to begin with the goal in mind."[2]

If you are trying to sell a recommendation, you will set up the presentation to support the plan. You will lay out your perspective and provide support points explaining why it makes sense. When you review the presentation, you will consider whether the document is clear and convincing. You will ask yourself these questions: Does this presentation sell the recommendation? Does it get the job done? You have a clear task to accomplish and a tight definition of success.

If you are simply providing an update on a project, you will write a very different type of presentation. You will gather data, organize it, and highlight important conclusions and implications. Your goal is to communicate information rather than sell a particular set of next steps.

Every presentation should have a purpose. I call this *purposeful presenting*. You never just present for the sake of presenting. There is always a reason, a point for the gathering. Being clear on this reduces the risk of wasting people's time and losing their attention.

First Things First

Some people get right to the task. Once they schedule the presentation time, they get busy creating pages and laying out the deck. These people believe procrastination is the enemy. They take joy from getting a quick start.

We tend to admire people like this. "I wish I had that sort of focus and energy!" we might think. Getting a draft done seems comforting and feels productive.

The problem is that you can't write a great presentation until you know what you are presenting. You have to know your message before you get started, so make sure you understand your goal before you begin putting your presentation together.

One of the simplest ways to get into trouble when working on a presentation is to start creating the actual document too early in the process. Unfortunately, this happens all the time. Someone schedules an executive update a week or two in advance, then the responsible team gets to work.

The first step, they think, is to develop a draft. So the team sits down and begins pulling together pages. They grab this chart and that chart and put them in a rough order. Before long, the presentation takes shape. There is heft to it and substance. It feels like it is really coming along.

The problem, of course, is that in many cases the objective—the message—isn't clear. What *is* the recommendation, anyway? Are we proposing to launch a new product? Are we suggesting we increase the price? Or should we decrease the price?

Without knowing the objective, the document is just a collection of facts. It doesn't make a point, because there is no point to make. There are charts and graphics, but there is no overall story. The document bloats. *Wall Street Journal* columnist Peggy Noonan notes, "When you don't know what you're saying, you take a long time to say it. When you know what you are saying, you get pithy. Audiences know this."[3]

Writing a presentation without knowing the objective is like driving without a destination. You only feel like you are making progress.

You get started on your long drive and then call your friend, "Hey, Bob, I'm making great time!"

He replies logically enough, "That's great! So where you are heading?"

"I have no idea. But the good news is that there isn't any traffic!"

A collection of facts is not a good presentation. It is just a collection of facts. It has little value. A collection of charts and graphs with no direction is actually worse than having no pages at all, because once you put a chart in a presentation, it is very difficult to take it out. It is tough to cut an analysis, so you justify its inclusion. You think, "This is such a neat segmentation analysis. Look at that: the nine purchase groups, and the three attitudinal groups." Even though the analysis may contribute nothing to the presentation, you leave it in.

So the first step in developing a presentation is to be clear on the recommendation. What is the point of the meeting? What is my message? What are my goals for the discussion? What do I want my audience to think, feel or do? Being clear on these questions will ensure that you write a presentation with purpose.

As legendary Roman orator Cato said many years ago, "Find the message first and the words will follow."[4]

A New Strategy for Kraft BBQ Sauce

One of the most challenging presentations I had to deliver in my career at Kraft was to recommend a restage of the Kraft BBQ Sauce business. At the time, Kraft BBQ was doing well financially; revenue, share and profit were growing. The overall financial metrics all looked healthy.

The problem was that the growth of Kraft BBQ was due to a combination of cost reduction products and deep promoted pricing. Historically, we had sold a bottle of Kraft BBQ Sauce around Memorial Day and July 4—the two big summer holidays in the United States—for 79 cents. Three years earlier, the Kraft BBQ brand manager decided that it would be a good idea to reduce the price to two bottles for 99 cents for the Memorial Day promotion event. This move generated a very large boost in revenue, share and profit.

The following year, in a bid to continue the growth trend, the BBQ team offered the deep discount price at both of the big holiday weeks: Memorial Day and July 4. This was another very successful year for the business, with additional revenue and profit growth.

The next year, the team dialed things up once again, now selling *three* bottles of Kraft BBQ Sauce for 99 cents at the big holidays. This generated yet another year of growth.

At the same time, product quality was falling due to a series of cost reduction projects; the team reduced the amount of tomatoes, molasses and spices in the formula and increased the amount of inexpensive ingredients such as water, vinegar and salt.

This was clearly an unsustainable path. Sales were up, but only because we were cutting the price. We were attracting price-sensitive customers, including a lot of people who simply used our sauce as a base—they doctored Kraft's sauce to get the precise flavor they wanted—but our brand preference was actually falling. People were buying Kraft BBQ, but their perceptions of the product were getting worse.

I took over the business at this time and quickly realized the business had to shift course. I worked with my team and developed a plan to improve product quality, cut back promotions, and invest in advertising and marketing. It was a solid plan. There was just one problem: it would lead to a sharp drop in revenue, share and profit. In the short run, results would fall as the price-driven customers left. In the long run, the business would be stronger but this would take time. You can't change people's perceptions of a brand overnight.

Selling this recommendation was not easy. I had to develop a presentation that explained the situation, projected the road ahead and then introduced the alternate plan. It wasn't a happy story; the business was in for a couple rough years.

Fortunately, I had a very clear objective heading into various meetings reviewing the plan: I had to get support for a risky and unpleasant but necessary strategic shift. Ultimately, I managed to work with my team and convince people it was the right course for the business.

5

KNOW YOUR AUDIENCE

PEOPLE ARE NOT all the same. We aren't robots or standardized mechanical devices. Some people like tomatoes and some people don't. Some people like numbers and some people don't. I like rodeos and county fairs. My wife doesn't.

This simple insight is at the heart of great marketing. There are so many differences between individual people that it is impossible to make everyone happy. If you try to delight all sorts of people, you will likely end up with a mediocre product or service, something that is adequate for everyone but perfect for no one. This will lead you to the bland middle where your product is just fine. Unfortunately, in a word full of competitive offerings, being fine is not enough.

To succeed, you can't be fine; you have to be outstanding. This is the only way to have an impact and get noticed. This means that you have to focus on a group of people with some common characteristics. If you are designing a perfect sandwich, you need to focus on carnivores or vegetarians. People who love onions or people who don't.

Picking and understanding your target is essential for success in marketing. It is one of the first lessons in a marketing class. It is also a tough concept to embrace—people don't like targeting.

The idea of targeting applies when you are presenting. People have different wants when it comes to presentations. It is highly unlikely that a presentation will be successful at reaching everyone. As psychotherapist Susan Dowell observes, "People have genuinely different ways of looking at things and interacting and you need to respect this right. Read their cues. Pay attention to how they talk about things." [1]

For this reason, you need to think about your audience before you start creating your presentation. It isn't enough to know what you are trying to communicate; you also have to know who you are presenting to and then consider what they want.

Presenting Is a Marketing Task

At the core, marketing is about understanding and interacting with customers. When you approach a task with a marketing lens, your focus shifts from the product to the customer. The question isn't "What am I selling?" or "What are my product attributes?" The question is "What do my customers want or need?" And "How can I help my customers achieve their goals?"

You can see the shift even when you are selling a basic product like a pencil. Your first instinct is to talk about the pencil. You might discuss the durable lead, the robust eraser or the bright color. These are all good points and notable product features.

With a marketing lens, the emphasis shifts; the focus isn't on the pencil but on the customer and their needs. So if my target is a business executive, I might talk about the productivity that comes from using a pencil or the power of quickly changing things with a good eraser. This could eventually lead me to a discussion about the importance of failure in the innovation process and the need to be resilient when dealing with challenges.

The same dynamic works with presentations. Your first instinct is to focus on the presentation itself: the text, the charts and the points you want to make. With a marketing lens, your perspective shifts. What does my target want to see? How do they want to see it?

Be Clear on Your Audience

One of the first tasks when developing a presentation is to clarify your target. Who is the most important person anyway? Is it Susan, Michael or Eduardo?

You need to zero in on a specific individual. Since people are different, you will struggle if you try to speak to multiple individuals at the same time. You want to identify the most important person you will be trying to reach.

There is always a most important person. Many times this will be the most senior individual. If you are presenting to the CEO of Lufthansa, you will think about the CEO. If you are presenting to the president of the United States, you will think about the president.

Sometimes the most important person in the meeting isn't the most senior. If you are trying to recruit new MBAs, for example, your key person will be your top prospect. The CEO might be at the presentation, but they aren't the primary target.

If you aren't clear on the key person, you likely aren't clear on the objective. What is the purpose of the meeting? When you define this, the target will usually become apparent.

Identify Their Preferences

Once you have clearly defined your target, you can get busy understanding them and figuring out what they want. This is an important step in the marketing world; if you don't understand your target, it is difficult to connect with them.

Consider your target's preferences. How do they like to review material? Is there a format or structure they prefer? People can have very different opinions. Companies vary, too, so it is useful to consider firm culture and norms.

HOW DO THEY FEEL ABOUT GROUPS?

People react differently to gatherings. Some people love large groups; others don't. If you are presenting to someone who is comfortable with a large audience, then you can present with this format. If your audience likes a small group, you'll want to present with just a few people.

Your goal is to make your audience comfortable so they can listen and then communicate. If someone is most at ease with a small group, putting them in the middle of a large group will make them nervous and stressed. They will be deliberate and careful about what they say. This is not a good way to get their support and honest feedback.

If your target likes large groups, on the other hand, then showing up with just two or three people might leave them disappointed or deflated. Where is the team? Why do we have such a small gathering?

I had two very different managers at Kraft Foods. One boss loved big meetings; he was an entertainer at heart. He spent much of the day telling Jerry Seinfeld jokes and making people laugh. He loved having an audience. Every day he would gather the team and take the group down to lunch, where he would preside over a lively meal. The best way to communicate with him was in a big room, packed with people. The more individuals in the room, the better. For this true showman, a large group was just another opportunity for him to shine.

Later, I had another manager who was very uncomfortable in large groups. He was a soft-spoken individual who tended to get particularly quiet when in a room with a lot of people. For this person, a small group discussion was the best approach. If you wanted to win him over and answer his questions, you had to keep the meeting very small. Five was a good number, perhaps six. Anything more than that was a problem.

ARE THEY READERS OR LISTENERS?

Some individuals like to read and some like to listen. As business strategist Peter Drucker observed, "Far too few people even know that there are readers and listeners and that people are rarely both."[2]

This is an important distinction. If people like to read, then you'll want to allow for this. You will write your presentation with the idea that it will be read first. You will get the document out early and give people a chance to review it before discussing.

If people like to listen, you should get right to the presentation. You will talk through your recommendation. You can assume people didn't and won't read your document outside of the meeting.

WHOM DO THEY TRUST?

Most people have a few individuals whom they trust and respect. Perhaps these people have worked together for a long time. Perhaps they have achieved success together. Maybe they went to the same school.

Whatever the bond, these work colleagues become very influential; if they recommend something, it may well get approved. If they frown or raise issues, the recommendation will probably lose momentum. It is important to identify these people and include them in the meeting. You will also want to presell them. If you can win over the influencers, you are well on your way to securing ultimate approval. At Kraft, the senior executives at our advertising agencies were usually well respected. For topics involving brand strategy and communication, it was essential to get them on board.

HOW DO THEY THINK?

People think in different ways. There is no one way to approach complex issues, and you should think about how your audience approaches them before writing a presentation.

One important distinction is inductive vs. deductive reasoning. You can determine how they think by asking yourself two simple questions: Do they like to see the data and then get to the conclusion? Or do they prefer to see the conclusion and then examine the supporting data?

If your audience likes to see the recommendation first, they will get very frustrated if you lead with the data. They might fidget in their chairs or flip ahead. They might ask, "Where is this all going?"

Alternatively, if your audience likes to get into the data, they will be uncomfortable if you start with the recommendation. They will feel like you are jumping the gun and will be anxious, eager to look at and study the information before reaching a conclusion.

Missing this distinction can set you up for a very painful presentation. You have to understand how they view things and how they consider problems. People also want different amounts of detail.

Some people want to see information—the more, the better. These people like nothing more than a page of business statistics. They pore over it, ask questions and look for the important trends.

If you are presenting to someone who loves data, you need to present data. A presentation that has great headlines and graphics but little information will go over poorly. A picture of a waterfall will add no value. If anything, it will just raise concerns. Where is the data? Your audience will be unhappy and unsatisfied.

Other people can be frustrated by data. If you show them a page full of numbers, they will skip by it and move on. A picture of a rainbow might work exceptionally well, dramatizing the power of a trend. Showing these people a lot of information is not just a waste of time; it will diminish your standing. One of my managers at Kraft had little patience for data. A rigorous, analytic presentation would often be met by "This is fine, but where are the ideas? Let's talk about ideas!"

Understand Their Priorities

One of the most important things to learn about life is that everyone has issues. We are all worried about something, all the time.

It is easy to lose track of this. You look at your colleague down the hall and think, "Wow, she really has it all. She just got promoted and she spoke at the big industry conference last week; she is supremely fit and has the nicest family. Her daughter just got into Stanford. I wish I had that sort of perfect life. Me? I can't even get to the gym once a week."

The reality isn't quite so clear. Your colleague is likely balancing all sorts of issues, just like you are. She might be facing a health issue or struggling with an inattentive spouse. She could be deeply worried about an upcoming project.

In a company, everyone has challenges, priorities and problems. This is true for the most junior clerk in the mail department and the CEO. They are just different challenges, priorities and problems. As Jeff Immelt, former CEO of GE, observes, "Every job looks easy when you're not the one doing it."[3]

As you head into the presentation, it is important to consider your audience. What are their priorities? If you know these, you can build a presentation that connects. Motivational speaker Tony Robbins starts with the audience, explaining, "My first thing in preparing for a presentation is you've got to know your audience and what their deepest needs are, their deepest desires, and their deepest concerns. That's more important than anything else."[4]

Consider the following questions:

HOW IMPORTANT IS THIS TOPIC?

Start with this! If this is an important topic, the audience will be engaged. They will want to see more information and detail and might be willing to help. Be ready.

If they don't really care about the topic, you will want to approach things differently. Assume they will check out in just a few minutes and plan on a brief presentation. They might get up and leave. If you need some help, think about how to grab their attention and then get to your recommendation or request.

You have to be honest about the situation. The presentation will surely be important for you. Anytime you are presenting to senior executives, you have an opportunity to advance or slow down your career.

The fact that a presentation is important to you doesn't mean your audience will really care. For example, I spent a lot of time in my career thinking about the correct price for Seven Seas salad dressing. The CEO of Kraft just didn't care; there were other, more important issues to address.

WHAT ARE THEIR GOALS?

It is critical to think about personal goals. What is important for your target?

If they want to show some quick results, then you should high-light how your plan will provide an easy win to boost the numbers. If your plan involves taking a hit to short-term profit, know that you will have a tough task.

If they are under pressure to make changes, make changes. Frame your recommendation as a fresh start. Use phrases like "It is time for a new approach" and "We have to change strategy" and "The current plan just isn't working."

WHAT ARE THEIR THEMES?

Business executives often embrace certain ideas; these form the core of the strategy. Someone might be thinking about reinvention, efficiency or disruptive innovation. If you can identify their theme, you can connect your recommendation to it. If your audience loves transformation, use the word "transformation" again and again.

When I worked for a manager who wanted innovation and fresh thinking, I talked about new ideas. In every presentation, I framed the recommendation as an innovation. I was innovating on promotions, advertising, packaging design and customer service. I had the most innovative team in the company. So much innovation. And the presentations generally went well.

Hostage negotiator Richard Mueller has used this approach successfully. He observes, "I don't persuade a person because I use my words; I persuade a person because I use theirs."[5]

Consider Their Perceptions

You need to consider your starting position. What is your target currently thinking about your situation? What are their perceptions?

We do this every time we tell someone a story; we provide information that builds on what people already know. If someone knows John is your colleague at work, you don't say, "I work with a fellow named John and yesterday..." If someone knows that you are working on a big new project, you don't say, "I just got put on this big new project at work, and you wouldn't believe what just happened..." Unconsciously, we assess what the person we are talking with knows and start from there.

This is also an essential question when developing a presentation. You need to understand where you stand before getting to work on the document.

HOW MUCH DO THEY KNOW?

One of the most important things to consider is how much your audience knows about a topic. If your audience is knowledgeable, you don't need to present a lot of background information. You can use industry jargon and show analyses with relatively little explanation.

A less informed audience will require a different approach. You will need to explain things in more depth. You should use jargon with care and explain different terms and calculations.

Getting this right is important. If you take someone with a lot of experience through basic industry information, they will be bored and frustrated. You might lose their support before you even get to the recommendation.

Moving quickly with a less experienced person is also a problem. They will likely be confused by your presentation. This will leave them with many questions and put them in a difficult spot. If they ask a lot of questions, they will slow down the meeting and look inexperienced. If they don't ask questions, they will simply be confused. Neither option is good.

Understanding what your audience knows isn't easy; you have to put yourself in their shoes. Harvard professor Steven Pinker, in his book *The Sense of Style*, calls this the "curse of knowledge." He describes it as "a difficulty in imagining what it is like for someone else not to know what you know." It is a particular challenge because we don't *know* what we don't know. Pinker explains it, "Like a drunk who is too impaired to realize that he is too impaired to drive, we do not notice the curse because the curse prevents us from noticing it."[6]

IT IS USEFUL to consider some basic questions when evaluating how much a particular executive might know:

- How long have they been responsible for the business?
- When did we last provide an update and what did we cover?
- What reports have they seen over the past few weeks?
- Who else have they heard from?

DO THEY ALREADY HAVE AN OPINION?

This is another critical question! If you are going to talk to someone about a particular issue, you need to know if they already have a point of view about the topic. This insight will have a major impact on how you proceed.

For example, if you are presenting to someone who agrees with your recommendation, you are simply working to confirm what they already understand and believe. If you are talking to someone who doesn't agree, you have a much different task. You have to shift their opinion and win them over.

Even the basic structure of your presentation will vary based on your audience's beliefs. If you are speaking to someone who agrees with you, you should quickly get to the recommendation. They will agree with it. The longer you wait, the more frustrated they will probably become. If your audience disagrees with your position, then this approach won't work; you are better off presenting different options and comparing the alternatives in order to sort out which one is best.

Do Your Research

Understanding a target isn't easy. You will probably have to work a bit to sort things out. You will need to do some research before the event.

One useful way to understand a senior executive is to talk to someone on their team. You might say, "So, Monica, I'm presenting to Angela next week on the new product launch. Any advice on presenting to Angela? What does she like?"

You can also simply ask the senior executive. If you have a chance to meet with the vice president before your meeting, you can inquire, "What do you like to see in a presentation?"

Be careful with this approach. Often, people don't actually know what they want, or they don't want what they think they want, and what they think they want they don't want. This is one of the challenges of marketing.

For this reason, it is sometimes more helpful to ask someone for an example. Just ask the question "Can you show me an example of a presentation you thought worked particularly well?" This will give you some material to work with. What is the structure of the deck? How much detail is given? Is it short or long?

Perhaps the best approach is to simply observe your target. Look at what people do, not what they say. What do they seem to like? When do they get frustrated and annoyed? What do their presentations look like?

To be a great presenter, you have to know your target. And to do this, you need to become a student of the craft, constantly observing, noting and learning.

Create a Presentation Brief

Before developing a new piece of advertising, advertisers write a creative brief. This document concisely summarizes the task. While there are many formats for these documents, they all generally include something about the objective, the target and the message.

The same approach can be very useful when working on a presentation. A presentation brief pulls together several elements:

- Objective: What is the goal of the meeting? Why are you writing this presentation anyway?
- Audience: Who is the key decision maker for this presentation? What do we know about this person in terms of their preferences, priorities and perceptions? Who else will be involved in the meeting?

- Format: How much time do we have? Where will the meeting be held? Will this be on-site or off-site?
- Other Considerations: What other factors do we need to consider? Is this a particularly controversial topic? Is timing tight, such that we need to come to a final decision at the meeting?

A presentation brief might look like this:

Exhibit 5-1 Example of a Presentation Brief

Objective	Gain agreement to everyday low-price strategy
Audience	**Susan Wellington,** Executive Vice President of Grocery Products Division • Usually runs late, is tight on time, wants to read the deck in advance • Is under pressure to deliver good results this year • Is very familiar with the business • Knows about the plan and is generally supportive **Markus Oakdale,** Head of Sales for Grocery Products Division • Strong supporter of the idea • Not too familiar with the financials
Format	One-hour meeting in the corporate boardroom
Considerations	Need a final decision at the meeting Should have presenters from marketing, finance and sales

6

FIVE THINGS EVERY PRESENTATION NEEDS

THERE ARE A few things every presentation should have. These are basic elements. You can avoid a lot of problems by making sure your presentations always have these five components.

1—Cover Page

Put a nice cover page on the presentation! This is a simple addition, but it adds considerable value in two ways.

First, a title page is an easy way to dress up a presentation. It signals that you care, that you took the time to make the presentation look good. It adds a bit of polish. As my Kellogg colleague Craig Wortmann observed in a recent class, "Luxury products come in beautiful packages."

Second, from a practical standpoint, you'll need a title page to show as you begin your delivery. It always takes a minute or two to get settled—this is the time for the title page.

A title page should include several specific elements.

TITLE

This is the topic. In general, the title of a presentation should reflect the content. If the focus is on pricing, then the title should be something related to pricing.

There are two things to consider when it comes to headlines.

The first is neutrality. You don't always want to lead with your recommendation; you only want to do this if you are confident that your audience is on board. Making the title "Recommendation to Enter Brazilian Market" communicates your perspective quite clearly. If your audience doesn't like the idea, they will immediately begin attacking the recommendation. They will probably take a deep breath and review their objections, all the reasons why the Brazilian market is such a bad opportunity. A more generic headline, such as "Brazilian Market Analysis and Recommendation," will reduce the immediate reaction. It gives you time to lay out your thinking before getting to the potentially controversial recommendation.

The second thing to consider is privacy. You might want to use a code name for particularly sensitive presentations. Corporate intelligence is a key issue for many companies, and you increase the chance that a competitor will end up with a presentation if you put the title right on the front page. More important, you increase the chance that someone will save the file with a clear description. This makes it easy for an uninvited visitor to find it. A file name like "Brazil Entry Recommendation" telegraphs the content. When I was at Kraft Foods, for example, we called the effort to launch a new potato-salad dressing "Project Spud."

DATE

Put the date on the front page!

The date is always important, because there will usually be many versions of a presentation floating around an organization. People will meet to discuss a new product launch dozens of times. The Brazilian expansion project will be the subject of many, many meetings. A date makes it clear which version, or which update, this is.

It is easy to overlook the date because you don't need the date for the meeting itself. If people at the meeting need to know the date, they can just look at their phones. You will need the date later, when you look back—when you have five versions of one document and you want to find a particular draft of the presentation.

NAMES

One of the elements that many people forget to put on the title page is the names of the team that created the presentation. You always should answer this simple question: Who wrote this?

People frequently move around a big company. Some people get promoted, others get transferred and others leave to pursue new opportunities. As a result, the team working on a project in November might be very different than the team that worked on it in March. At the time of a presentation, it is often quite clear who is on the team. A few months later, the situation may have changed.

If you know who worked on a particular update, you can go back to ask them about key assumptions. You can also get information on how it went.

LOCATION

Many presentations will include the location on the cover page. This can be helpful to provide some context, although it isn't essential. For example, I don't typically put the location on the front page of my presentations at Kellogg, since the majority of them are in Evanston.

2—Purpose

It is always best to start a presentation with a statement of the purpose: What are we doing here? You can think of this as the destination check. Where is the airplane heading?

The purpose could be to

- review an annual marketing plan,
- discuss the latest business results or
- consider a new product recommendation.

There is always a purpose! Remember, one of the first things to sort out is the reason for the presentation. If you don't know why you are having a meeting, you shouldn't be presenting in the first place. Just cancel it and save the time.

Putting the purpose right up front is useful for both the presenter and the audience. For the presenter, it grounds the presentation and increases the chance that it will be focused. For the audience, it clarifies the goal of the meeting right at the beginning. As speaker Scott Berkun observes, "If it takes ten minutes to explain what your point is, something is very wrong." [1]

3—Agenda

Every presentation should have an agenda. This is a basic, simple rule. An agenda provides structure. It highlights what is coming when. It is a map for the presentation.

The agenda goes at the front of the presentation and shows the basic flow. It should generally reappear several times. If you have five items on the agenda, you will probably show the agenda six times: once to show the overall flow, and then five more times as you move into each section. With each section, you note where you are by putting a circle or square around the section. The agenda serves as a series of signposts.

The main reason to have an agenda is that it helps your audience to know what topics will be covered and when. This plays a critical role in setting up their expectations. When should they expect to see the recommendation? How many sections are there to get through? All of this will put your audience at ease. TED's Chris Anderson notes that it is critical to set the overall direction for a talk: "When the audience knows where you are headed, it's much easier for them to follow."[2]

You never want your audience to be unsettled. If they don't know that you have the agenda and flow worked out, they may well get antsy as you walk through an analysis of customer complaint trends in Japan over the past seven years.

I was in a presentation recently where there was no agenda. It was a major problem. The meeting was scheduled to last from 2 to 3 p.m. The presenters got started right on time, laying out an interesting review of the business. They took us through an impressive segmentation study and a competitive analysis. But then it was 2:30 and we still hadn't gotten to the recommendation.

And then 2:40 rolled around. I started to get a little nervous. I wondered, "When will we see the recommendation?" By 2:45 I was concerned, thinking, "Maybe there is no recommendation at all! Or did I schedule the wrong time for this?" At 2:50 I couldn't wait any longer—I jumped in and started asking questions.

It turns out the team did have a logical recommendation; the meeting was just running longer than anticipated. It didn't end well, though. We rushed through the recommendation, which resulted in a very frustrating finish. Not surprisingly, we didn't agree on anything. We just decided to meet again.

An agenda is also a useful tool for the presenter. Creating the agenda forces you to have a flow and structure to your presentation. If you have to lay out the sections, you have to think through what you are going to cover when. The simple process of writing an agenda ensures that there will be some logic and organization to the presentation. What comes first? What comes later?

Sometimes you will write the agenda and realize the entire presentation isn't going to work—there are too many sections, or the flow doesn't seem to make sense. This is useful feedback. It reduces the chance you'll move ahead with an ineffective presentation.

The agenda can also help you manage the time. If you see minutes slipping away while you are presenting the first section, you know you have a time problem. If you realize this early in the meeting, you can take steps to address it.

An agenda shouldn't be too long or too short. As Harvard's Steven Pinker notes, "Like all writing decisions, the amount of signposting requires judgment and compromise: too much, and the reader bogs down in reading the signposts; too little and she has no idea where she is being led."[3]

It doesn't make any sense to have an agenda with just one thing on it. What is the point? Even an agenda with two items seems rather modest. If this is the case, you will want to break up your argument into more sections.

You can't list too many items, either. An agenda with ten or fifteen things on it is just not going to work. It's too much. You might be covering too much in your presentation, or you are cutting things into sections that are too small.

If you find yourself with an exceptionally long agenda, you should consider splitting the topic into several different meetings. An agenda with fifteen items could turn into three agendas with five items each.

4—Executive Summary

Say this with me: "I will always have an executive summary." Now let's say it again: "I will always have an executive summary."

The reason why an executive summary is so important is simple: your audience is busy. They have a full plate of activities. They are worried about different issues, both at work and at home. They have a very limited attention span.

This means that you have a very narrow window in which to get through to your audience. How long? It might be just a few minutes. Then the distractions will appear. The CEO reaches for their smartphone and starts checking email. They talk to the person next to them. Worst case, they get up and leave.

A good executive summary highlights the key points. It recaps the presentation in just a few simple sentences. Most important, it states the point of the meeting. Remember Scott Berkun's advice: "If it takes ten minutes to explain what your point is, something is very wrong."[4]

In most cases, the executive summary will include the recommendation—communicate what you are going to cover and recommend right up front.

There are *some* situations where you might delay the recommendation. Instead of saying, "We recommend Plan A," you say, "There are two options to consider: Plan A and Plan B." Generally, you will take this approach if you know your audience will not support your recommendation. If the CEO loves Plan B and you are recommending Plan A, then you want to be careful how you approach the discussion. You may be better off building to the conclusion. Putting it right up front might put the CEO on the defensive.

An executive summary is incredibly useful for your audience. If they agree with the overall direction, they can tune out and focus on other things. If they have questions, they know where to focus.

An executive summary should generally be one page, with a headline and perhaps five or six bullet points. This forces you to be concise and distill the key points from your presentation. A three- or four-page summary doesn't really work; it has too much detail. By the time you get through the summary, the presentation itself will seem unnecessary.

The executive summary can go before or after the agenda. Leading off with it often works well; you first lay out your basic story and recommendation, and then you show how you will walk through it step-by-step.

The executive summary and agenda should be linked. If your first point is "Our business is performing exceptionally well," then it would make sense for the agenda to start with a section titled "State of the Business" where you explain how well the business is doing.

Some people like to write the executive summary at the beginning of the process. Other people prefer to write it at the end. In many cases, it ends up being a bit of a circular process; you do a draft and then come back later to revise it as the presentation takes shape.

5—Conclusion

You need to end the presentation on a solid note, and the best way to do this is with a strong conclusion page.

Without a final page, people don't really know that the presentation is done and the show is over. Great performances always end decisively. At the end of a movie, the credits appear. At the end of a play, the curtain closes. Singers usually save a great song for the finale and call out, "Thank you so much! We love you, Tokyo!" as they walk off the stage and the lights come up. All these steps tell the audience the production has ended. In most meeting rooms, there isn't a curtain to close. You can bring up the lights, but you don't run credits (though it could be nice: *Copying— Jon Phillips; Financial Analysis—Jennifer Simpson; Market Research Insights—Peter Kim; Lunch—David O'Reilly*).

Ending without a conclusion page can lead to an awkward moment when the presenter is standing, looking at the silent crowd. Or you might end up with an inspirational line, such as "Well, that concludes my presentation," or "Any questions?"

The final page is important whether the presentation has gone well or poorly. If it has been a successful presentation, you want to leave everyone nodding their heads. This is the time to really hit your points and seal the deal. If the presentation has been a struggle, the conclusion is your chance to frame the argument one last time and shed some light on what is coming next.

A good summary slide simply recaps the main points. It should be a short page; this is not the time for in-depth information. You shouldn't put financial data or market research findings on a summary page. Just list the main points you covered.

Remember that the conclusion slide is not the place to introduce new information, either. You don't want to drop in something like "And so we proposed a $22-billion acquisition" on the final slide as people are packing up and getting ready to head out.

Some people like to just run the executive summary slide from the beginning of the presentation again at the end. This simple approach can work well.

Another approach is to close with the next steps: What happens now? This is a good way to connect the presentation to action. If everyone at the meeting agrees that three things will now happen, there is a good chance that those three things will actually happen.

7

FIND THE STORY

NOW COMES THE task of actually building the presentation. This is the time when you start creating pages and putting together the slides. You lay out your case. This is the hard work. As Winston Churchill wrote, "The foundations have to be laid, the data assembled, and the premises must bear the weight of the conclusions."[1]

At the heart of a presentation is a story, a logical flow of ideas and information. Finding the flow isn't easy but it is perhaps the most important step when it comes to presenting. Communications coach Carmine Gallo notes, "Creating the story, the plot, is the first step to selling your ideas with power, persuasion and charisma. Succeeding at this step separates mediocre communicators from extraordinary ones."[2]

With a strong flow, a presentation will work. One page will logically lead to the next page. It will feel intuitive and natural. Questions will come up and then be answered. Your audience will follow along, nodding. It will seem easy, and this will help you sell your recommendation. As psychologist Daniel Kahneman notes, "When you are in a state of cognitive ease, you are probably in a good mood, like what you see, believe what you hear, trust your intuitions, and feel that the current situation is comfortably familiar."[3]

A weak flow, on the other hand, leads to a difficult presentation. With tenuous connections from page to page, the presentation feels scattered. Your audience will be searching for information, flipping ahead or looking back.

Getting the right structure is essential for a strong presentation, much like getting the framing right is important when constructing a house. "If you're trying to make a case on the page, at a presentation or in giving a formal speech, structure is something that you need to be intensely interested in," observes Sam Leith, a columnist at the *Financial Times*.[4]

Finding the story isn't easy. Life is complicated. The issues facing a business can have multiple dimensions. There is a remarkable amount of data to work with. Turning a complex situation into a simple story requires real effort.

A Presentation Is a Story

The best way to identify the flow for your presentation is to think of it as a story. You aren't presenting information and data; you are telling someone a tale about the business.

People naturally tell stories; this is what humans have been doing for thousands of years. "You just let the speaker take you on a journey, one step at a time. Thanks to our long history around campfires, our minds are really good at tracking along," notes TED's Chris Anderson.[5] Presentation expert Nancy Duarte agrees, explaining in her 2011 TED talk, "There's something kind of magical about a story structure."[6]

With a good story, things feel logical. Points build from one to the next. It moves along. It is interesting.

Consider a story like this:

Did you hear what happened yesterday? Peter was late for school, so he was speeding down Main Street. When he turned onto Union Street, a policeman saw him. Instead of stopping, Peter just took off. Crazy, right?

He headed down Union Street, took a quick turn on Pleasant Avenue and then looped around to the high school. The policeman was right behind him, lights flashing, so he tried to cut through the shopping plaza. But another officer cut him off. He was arrested and is in real trouble. I don't know what he is going to do!

The story feels natural. It starts with an introduction, then leads to the situation. There is a sequence of events. The sentences connect, one to the next. There is enough information. There aren't random, unrelated facts. This is a strong story.

Now consider this one:

Peter drove to school today. I think he was driving his father's old Buick. You remember that old car? It is blue and pretty scratched up. I drove in it last month; I think we went out for lunch. It might have been to Wendy's. Don't you like the burgers at Wendy's? He was late so he was speeding. I usually try to stay under the speed limit so I don't get a ticket. Have you ever gotten a ticket? I got one last week. One hundred dollars! That is so frustrating; I really can't afford a ticket, especially because my clutch is going bad. Do you know how much it costs to fix a clutch? A policeman saw Peter and chased him to school. Who do you think is going to win the football game on Saturday?

This is the same story, only now the flow is chopped up. There is a lot of random, scattered and irrelevant information. It is hard to figure out where the story is going or what to pay attention to. What was the point here, anyway? It simply doesn't work as a narrative.

Finding the Flow

To find your story, it is useful to think about several things.

BEGIN WITH THE KEY POINTS

Start by thinking about the key points. What are you trying to get across? In most cases, this will relate to your objective.

At this stage, you should ignore the detailed data; your focus should be the significant points. For example, "Sales are growing quickly" is an important point. "Sales are up by 7.8 percent" is more detail than you need at this step in the process. Later, you will need specific data to support your argument. You will need charts and graphs. This is not the time.

Jonathan Copulsky, former CMO of Deloitte, draws a distinction between horizontal and vertical logic in a presentation. Horizontal logic is the flow of the pages. Vertical logic is the structure of each page. As you work on the story, focus on the horizontal logic. You shouldn't worry about the details on a particular page until you know it is going to be in the final document.

Your goal is to find the correct sequence of points. Remember that, ultimately, the flow of points should lead to your recommendation.

DEFINE THE START

The first question is the start. Where should the presentation begin? One of your initial steps should be sorting this out. As Nancy Duarte notes, "At the beginning of any presentation you need to establish what is. You know, here's the status quo. Here's what's going on."[7]

In most cases, you don't want to go too far back in time. If you start a presentation by saying, "In 1972, our business was performing well, with share, revenue and profit all growing nicely," then you have a big task ahead; you have to go through all the developments since 1972. Now, it could be that the roots of the situation indeed go back that far, so it is the only logical place you can start. Otherwise you'll want to start with the current situation or the very recent past.

Your starting point should reflect your key audience member. If you are presenting to the CEO, think about what they know. What did you say last time you saw them? What have they heard in the meantime?

If you've been providing weekly updates on your business, your story shouldn't start three years ago; you've already told this part of the story. You don't need to go through it all again.

If your audience doesn't know much about your business, however, then a bit of history might be useful to provide some perspective on the situation.

Remember that your audience may well have forgotten what you talked about in the last meeting or need a bit of a reminder. Most business executives are bombarded with information and reports these days, so it can be tough to recall the specific situation on a business. Worst case, a quick reminder of the situation will get you off to a solid start. Just watch your audience; if they are ready to move on, then move on!

ANSWER THE LOGICAL QUESTIONS

Your presentation should then logically flow from your starting point. What would be a natural question? For example, if you start a presentation by saying, "We introduced the new 948 polymer in April," then a natural question might be "How is it doing?" or "How did we support the launch?"

This initial question will drive the entire flow of the presentation, so spend time thinking about it. You might say, "Last year was a great year for the business," or "Results in Q3 were concerning," or "Digital platforms are growing at a remarkable pace." Each statement will begin a different story.

DON'T CREATE A LIST

Remember that a story is not a list. The goal is to move forward from one point to the next, not to walk through a lot of data.

Lists are easy to develop but hard to remember. It isn't hard to write down a list of ten things. Try creating these lists: "Ten Foods I Enjoy," "Six Places I've Been on Vacation" and "Things I Am Afraid Of." It is an easy task. Of course, if you show the list to someone, they will probably forget most of the items rather quickly.

A story is more powerful and memorable, and more difficult. As screenwriter Robert McKee notes, "Any intelligent person can sit down and make lists. Persuading with a story is hard."[8]

Two Techniques

There are many different ways to develop a story. Two common techniques are speaking first and storyboarding.

SPEAK, THEN WRITE

One of the simplest ways to find the narrative flow is to simply tell someone the story, and then write it down.

The insight behind this approach is that people are naturally better at speaking than writing. Speaking is intuitive. Almost everyone talks and tells stories. Charles Darwin noticed this, observing, "Man has an instinctive tendency to speak, as we see in the babble of our young children, whereas no child has an instinctive tendency to bake, brew or write."[9]

When we tell a story, we are providing a sequence of information. This is the structure of the presentation. The more a presentation is like a natural conversation, the better it will work. Author Geoffrey James embraces the speaking approach: "The trick to simplifying your communication is: write the way you talk. In my experience, almost everybody is better at talking clearly than at writing clearly." [10] Cary Lemkowitz recommends the same approach in his book: "Think of the audience as children, and tell them a story." [11]

There are different ways to do this. One is to record yourself speaking; just talk through the story and later write down what you covered. Another is to tell someone the story, and let them note the order of the points. Either approach can work well.

STORYBOARD

One of the best ways to lay out a story is to develop a storyboard. This is the process of mapping out how the various pages will flow in the presentation.

To create a storyboard, you simply take a piece of paper and draw three vertical lines and three horizontal lines, creating nine squares. Each square then represents a page in the presentation. You can also create the boxes on the computer. It will look like this:

Exhibit 7-1

You then write the page headline at the top of each box, and perhaps some indication of what might be on the page below. You might have a headline with a bar chart below, or a headline with some bullets. Often it works best to simply write in the headlines; there is no need to worry about typing or formatting.

Filled out, it might look like this:

Exhibit 7-2

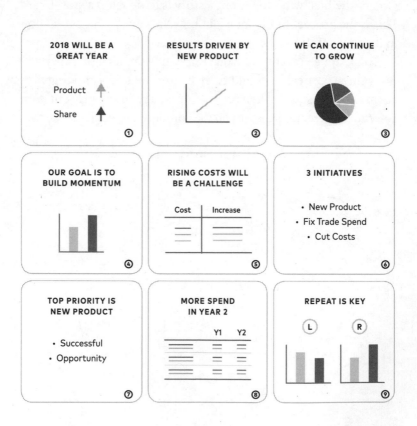

It is best to use a pencil when doing this. You can then easily move things around; just erase one headline and move it to another box. I don't use the computer when developing the story; for some reason I find that it makes it more difficult to move things around. Communications coach Carmine Gallo shares this perspective. He writes, "Whether you plan best on a white board, a yellow legal pad, or Post-it notes, spend time in analog before jumping to digital." [12]

You don't want much detail on the pages; it should be very rough. In Exhibit 7-2, some pages have just four or five words. This makes it easy to move the pages around; there isn't much to erase. In addition, you have nothing invested in the pages, so you don't feel bad cutting pages or even complete sections.

It is rare that you will nail a story on the first try; in most cases you will lay out a story, and then change it, and then change it again

This is where the hard work of writing a presentation occurs. Some executives spend hours working on the presentation flow, moving things around and debating the flow.

Structures to Consider

There are many ways to structure a presentation; there isn't one set format, just as there isn't just one way to tell a story. As Steven Pinker notes, "The ways to order material are as plentiful as there are ways to tell a story." [13] How you organize a presentation should depend on the recommendation, the data and your audience.

Many presentations follow one of several structures; it is worth considering these as you begin laying out your case and looking for the flow.

CHRONOLOGICAL

The simplest way to develop a presentation is to use time; one development flows to the next. You start at a moment and then progress forward. The flow ends with the conclusion or recommendation.

The flow might look like this:

- We introduced our new drill lubricant in 2015.
- The goal was to drive incremental profits by entering an attractive category.
- We supported the launch with a major marketing investment.
- Results exceeded our expectations in 2015 and 2016.
- Based on this, we expanded the product line and added two new items in 2017.
- These have been very well received and the business continued to grow in 2018.
- To further our growth, we recommend launching an additional two items.

With this structure, you are telling a story, explaining step-by-step what has happened and why.

The appeal of this design is that it is easy to follow; people naturally understand the approach. It also creates some drama; the flow of the story can pull people along through it.

The challenge with a chronological approach is that it is easy to get lost in the details. You will be tempted to include all the various twists and turns that the business has encountered. Much of this information is probably not relevant or important; you have to be disciplined about cutting extraneous information.

PROS AND CONS

People have been debating for years; it is one of the core ways people communicate. In a debate, people hear two sides; one person argues for one side of an issue, and another person argues for the other side.

This approach can be a fine structure for a presentation: you set up a debate topic and then explore the two sides, eventually arriving at your conclusion.

It could look like this:

- Today we want to consider the introduction of two new products.

- There are some compelling reasons to introduce these items:
  - The items will address an underserved segment.
  - The launch will generate excitement.
  - The financials look good.

- There are also concerns, reasons to not launch the new products:
  - Developing the items will take R&D resources.
  - Competitors might respond aggressively.
  - It will increase complexity for our sales organization.

- On balance, we believe the argument favors the introduction.

The power of this approach is that it is simple and focused. It works particularly well if you have one main question to consider with just two or three possible outcomes; it won't work for a more ambiguous situation where there are many different possible paths forward.

The challenge with a pros-and-cons structure is that you have to build it with great thought. If you are too effective at arguing for the other side, you can inadvertently convince people to actually oppose your recommendation. Instead of getting agreement, it can just solidify the debate. Partly for this reason, some people dislike this approach. Use it with care!

ISSUE-SOLUTION

With this structure, you present an issue and then present a solution. Barbara Minto, in her book *The Pyramid Principle,* refers to this as "situation-complication-solution" structure; you start with a noncontroversial statement, then highlight an issue or a potential issue, then discuss how to address it.[14] The beauty of this structure is that you get right to the point. It creates urgency, especially if you present the issue with energy.

It might look like this:

- Our drill lubricant business has been performing well. (Situation)

- There are major challenges ahead. (Complication)
    - The category is flattening.
    - Our market share is stable.
    - As a result, our growth is slowing.
    - There is little chance these trends will change soon.

- To address this problem, we recommend launching two new items. (Solution)
    - These items will address a gap in the market.
    - They will create excitement within our sales organization.
    - The move will address the growth challenge.

The issue-solution structure is perhaps the most direct approach for a presentation; you highlight a problem or opportunity, and then provide a solution to that problem. It can be a compelling call to action; if the situation is highly concerning, your audience will be motivated to do something in response.

Watch the Beginning and the End

I have long believed that presentations are a bit like airplane flights.

There are basically three parts to a flight: takeoff, cruising and landing. The most dangerous parts of the flight are the takeoff and the landing, in part because the plane is close to the ground.

When cruising along at 38,000 feet, a bit of turbulence isn't a major concern; the plane can bounce as it flies along. Only the most severe types of turbulence pose a major hazard. When taking off, however, turbulence is a more significant concern. Dropping a quick fifty feet is a rather big issue if you are only thirty feet off the ground.

For this reason, pilots have to be particularly attentive during takeoff and landing. You don't usually see your pilot coming out looking for a cup of coffee as the plane heads down the runway, and you don't see a pilot chatting with the flight attendants during the final approach. During the cruising section, the situation is very different. Pilots wander around. They have dinner, drink coffee and, I suspect, talk about the weekend and plans for the upcoming layover.

Presentations have the same three parts: takeoff, cruising and landing. The takeoff is the first few minutes of the presentation, when you are just getting going. The cruising section is the bulk of the presentation time. The landing is the conclusion.

Just like flight, the takeoff and landing are the most important and dangerous parts of a presentation. The start of a meeting really matters; it sets the tone. Most important, the beginning can have a huge impact on your energy. If you get off to a solid start, you will feel confident and secure. This will propel you forward. Your audience will relax, too. If you get off to a rough start, however, things can rapidly spiral down. You might be nervous and insecure. Worst case, your audience may decide that the entire presentation is suspect and then tune out everything you have to say.

It is important to capitalize on this insight when constructing a presentation. At the beginning, you want to cover easy material. This is not the time for controversial statements or complex analyses. You want to present material that people will understand and agree with. You might recap agreements from a prior discussion or show business results that people are aware of, information that is consistent with the general perspective.

Putting familiar, easy material at the start will get your audience nodding along. This is the right frame of mind. Once you've gotten into the presentation, once you have a bit of momentum and altitude, you can begin going through more complex and difficult material. You can handle some tough questions at this stage in the meeting.

The closing, too, is important. The best presentation in the world will have no impact if things go wrong at the end. You want your last few slides to be easy. You certainly don't want to put a difficult recommendation at the very end. This might damage the entire presentation. It could also anger your audience; it might look like you are trying to hide the material by putting it very late. You need to close by locking down the agreements and setting the course for next steps.

Revise, Rework and Tighten

Developing a logical story is hard work. To create a tight flow, you will need to go through it again and again, checking the flow. Business leadership coach Steven Robbins recommends you start by getting a rough version complete. "Keep moving forward. Yes, you'll have sentence fragments. You'll have misspellings, and you'll have somewhat fractured logic. That's nice. You'll fix it later." Then you should rework the entire presentation: "Start at the top and go through, demolishing it. Cut, paste, rewrite. Shorten, lengthen, and wordsmith." [15]

Seasoned executives understand the need to rework and revise. Jim Kilts, CEO of corporations such as Kraft, Nabisco and Gillette, would revise an important presentation fifty or sixty times before settling on a final version. Jack Welch, former CEO of GE, loved the challenge of getting the story precisely right: "For every analyst meeting, I'd sit for hours with my finance and investor relations team, sketching out and tearing up chart after chart." [16]

As you work on the flow, you should ask yourself several questions:

DO WE NEED THIS PAGE?

Here is a simple rule: if you don't need a particular page in a presentation, you should drop it. Every page should have a function and contribute to the larger story.

In general, shorter presentations are better than longer ones, so you should cut everything that isn't essential. If you have a page that doesn't make an important point, drop it. If a piece of information isn't critical to the discussion, prune it. You don't want to waste your audience's time. As advertising executive Bob Rehak notes, "Respect readers' time and readers may become more interested." He advises, "Keep boiling down your argument until it is easy to understand and you're not wasting a single word." [17]

Don't take this to an extreme. You need enough pages to communicate the information clearly and logically. Sometimes more pages will be better than fewer pages. If you are building a complex analysis, you may want to introduce it piece by piece.

Be particularly careful with page targets. Setting a specific page limit makes no sense at all.

IS THERE TOO MUCH MATERIAL ON THE PAGE?

One of the most common presentation problems is clutter. On a single page you might find a bar chart, a set of bullet points and a two-by-two matrix. This just doesn't work well. What is important? Where is a reader supposed to look?

Each page in a presentation should make one point. There should be a single idea, supported with data or visuals. If you have a page with multiple points, you should split it into two pages, or even more.

It is better to have more pages that logically work together than fewer, cluttered pages. A twenty-page presentation that is clear and simple is much better than a four-page presentation that has cluttered pages, no story and no flow.

You can have several items on a particular page; there is nothing wrong with a line chart together with three bullet points. The key is that the information should work together. It should be clear why the information is on the same page.

DOES ONE PAGE FLOW TO THE NEXT?

In a good presentation, the pages should flow naturally; it should all feel logical. It is just like you are telling a story. If you say, "I had a great weekend," you should probably then say, "I went to the movies," and then "I saw *Wonder Woman*." This is obvious when thinking about a conversation.

The dynamic is also important when it comes to presentations. If you say, "Sales were up 18 percent last year," the next page should probably explain why. If you have a page describing the new product development effort you implemented over the last year, you might then have a page reviewing the results.

One way to test the flow is to ask yourself what your audience might be thinking about after a page. If you say, "We are worried about rising interest rates," a logical person might wonder why, or how likely an increase really is.

DO I MOVE TO THE CONCLUSION?

Ultimately, you need to get to and support your recommendation. A series of interesting points might engage the audience, but it won't be a successful meeting if you don't get to the point.

So, as you look at the flow of a presentation, you should check that it is moving you in the right direction. Does this presentation naturally take me to the recommendation?

Best case, a presentation will arrive at the recommendation in a completely natural manner. The proposed solution will seem like an obvious solution. Your audience will think, "Of course! Doing anything else would make little sense."

ARE THE PAGES MECE?

When constructing a presentation, the points should be MECE. This phrase, used frequently by consulting firms when developing recommendations, means "mutually exclusive, collectively exhaustive." Both parts of this are important.

"Mutually exclusive (ME)" means that each point should be different. You shouldn't just repeat the same thing; this is redundant and tiresome. For example, don't say, "Our key target is suburban soccer moms," and then "Suburban soccer moms are an important target." This is just repeating yourself; it makes your presentation longer and more complex than necessary.

The phrase "collectively exhaustive (CE)" is also important; it means that your presentation should be complete. It should touch on all the key points. If there is a critical issue, the presentation should address it.

Spend the Time

This phase of the process can be frustrating. It takes a long time and progress will seem limited. You aren't creating pages and polishing charts. You may think, "I've spent five hours on this and I don't even have a single page done yet. All I have is a pile of Post-it notes."

Don't be discouraged! It takes time to create a strong story, but it is an investment that will pay back many times over. If the presentation flow works, then the presentation is set up for success.

8

CREATE SIMPLE
PAGES

ONCE YOU HAVE the overall structure of a presentation set, you can turn to creating the actual pages. This is when you put words to paper: you write headlines and add tables and charts.

Wait

People love this part of the process because they feel like they are making real progress on the task. They can see the pages take shape. There is tangible output.

It is tempting to jump directly to this stage. Creating pages feels significant. If you have fifteen PowerPoint pages complete, it seems that you are well underway. You've made real progress!

Don't do it.

You can't start the task of creating pages until you know the overall flow of the presentation. One page has to connect to the next page; each slide is like a piece of a puzzle. This means that you can only create an effective page if you know how it fits into the flow; you have to know the previous page and the following page.

Create a Strong Headline

The most important element on a page is the headline. This is where you state the main point. The headline should be crisp and clear. If the headline works, the page will likely work.

When you developed the overall story, you probably had the first draft of a headline. If you created a storyboard, you presumably wrote in a first version. As you now construct the page, you should go back to revisit this. Is the phrasing correct? Does the language work? Very often you captured just an idea in the previous phase. Now you have to make sure the idea comes across as an effective headline.

Remember that one headline should flow to the next. One way to check your presentation is to go through it, reading only the headlines. Ideally, these should form a natural story; someone should be able to understand the presentation by looking at just the headlines.

MAKE IT A SENTENCE

A good headline states the conclusion, or the main point. It doesn't just say what is on the page. It should be a sentence, complete with a subject and a verb. There should be a main point to the headline. Remember, you are telling a story, not just communicating data.

The following headlines add very little value:

- Sales by Region
- Customer Segmentation
- Margin Trends
- Net Promoter Score

- Stage-Gate Process Update
- Results by Quarter

These are all fine things, but they are not effective headlines. When you read "sales by region," you don't learn anything. You can assume that the information is accurate, but why does it matter? What is the point of the page? What does "sales by region" tell us?

A title like "sales by region" shows that you are just presenting data. This is probably a waste of time. Why bother to create a presentation at all? Just print out the charts and send them over, or just send the spreadsheet.

Presenting data adds little value. Worse, people might interpret the information in different ways. This can be a problem. Your goal is to sell a recommendation; you want to shape how people view a situation and guide them to a conclusion.

A good presentation involves synthesis and analysis. You aren't just showing someone information; you are making sense of it, working with it, forming it into a compelling argument. There is too much information in the world; nobody needs a presentation that simply gives them more of it.

With a headline, you want the point to come across. Why do we care? The headlines above would add much more value if rephrased:

Don't write: "Sales by Region"
Write: "The West Region is critical for our business."

Don't write: "Customer Segmentation"
Write: "The 'Eager Shoppers' segment is our key target."

Don't write: "Margin Trends"
Write: "We grew our margins significantly last year."

Don't write: "Net Promoter Score"
Write: "Our net promoter score has been increasing."

Turning a headline into a sentence with a subject and an action will help ensure that each page has a point.

LIMIT THE HEADLINE TO TWO LINES

A headline shouldn't be long. The best headlines are one or two lines; these are easy to read and understand.

Longer headlines don't work well. A three-line headline, for example, is simply too much. In part this is because a three-line headline is visually difficult to read. More important, a three-line headline means you haven't really summarized the key point; you still have distilling to do.

If your headline is too long, you should rewrite it and simplify it. Shrinking the type size or changing the type font is not a solution; these should be consistent on every page. You have to tighten the idea.

Long headlines sometimes indicate that you have too much information on the page. Splitting the material into two pages may address the problem. A headline like "Sales are declining in three of four regions. The East Region is increasing due to better distribution and sales coverage" would easily split into two pages, with one headline being "Sales are declining in three of four regions. Only the East Region is growing" and the other being "The East Region is growing due to better distribution and sales coverage."

MAINTAIN PARALLEL STRUCTURE

Every headline in a presentation should be similar in structure. Best case, all of the headlines are short sentences.

Parallel structure ensures that the presentation will work well in its entirety. It feels polished and professional. The following collection of statements works; each one is a complete sentence.

There is parallel construction:

- Sales have declined sharply over the past year.
- The decline in sales is due to a drop in buying rate.
- The penetration rate has remained stable even as the buying rate has declined.
- We can connect the drop in buying rate to fewer purchases per occasion.

Changing structure creates a sense of discontinuity in the presentation. A presentation that lacks parallel structure isn't polished. For example, this next mix of sentences and phrases is a jumble; there is no consistent structure or format:

- Sales by year
- Sales are down due to a fall in buying rate.
- Growing customer penetration
- Regional revenues
- We can connect the drop in buying rate to fewer purchases per occasion.

The result is that the presentation does not seem polished.

INCLUDE TRANSITIONS

It is good to use transition words and phrases to connect pages in the presentation. Using "as a result" and "on the other hand" and "in addition" strengthens the flow. Remember, headlines taken together should form a story.

A flow of headlines like this works well:

Our sales grew by 8 percent last year.
However, profits fell by 9 percent.
This key challenge was a decline in variable margin.
The margin decline was due to an increase in product cost ...

... and a jump in variable labor rates.

As a result, reducing costs is a key priority.

In this sequence, each headline has a role. There are transitions along the way to connect one point to the next. As Natalie Canavor, author of *Business Writing in the Digital Age*, notes, "Good transitions create the binding that holds your piece together and reinforces the logic of your argument."[1]

AVOID THE PASSIVE VOICE

Don't write in the passive voice! This is true throughout your presentation, but it is particularly important when it comes to writing headlines.

The passive voice occurs when you turn the object of an action into the subject. It looks like this:

Active Voice: "We launched a new brand of shaving cream."
Passive Voice: "A new brand of shaving create was launched."

Active Voice: "We increased profits by 22 percent."
Passive Voice: "Profits were increased by 22 percent."

Active Voice: "Our key competitor launched a new ad campaign."
Passive Voice: "A new ad campaign was launched."

IT IS ALWAYS better to write in the active voice and avoid the passive voice. There are three problems with passive writing. First, it lacks energy. It feels flat and it doesn't communicate excitement. When you write, "A pricing strategy change was made," you don't generate real interest. It is far better to write "We changed our pricing strategy."

Second, passive writing isn't clear. There is no obvious actor. Who launched the new ad campaign, anyway? Who changed the pricing? Did it just happen on its own? It is much better to include the actor.

Third, passive writing avoids ownership. When you say "A new brand of shaving create was launched," you are distancing yourself from the action. You are not taking responsibility.

Senior executives want people to take ownership. Writing in the passive voice suggests you aren't having an impact. Things are just happening. James Humes, the Ryals Professor of Language and Leadership at the University of Southern Colorado and the author of several books on language, writes, "The passive is for the 'cover-your-ass' types. The passive is not the voice of a leader. The passive is the voice of the bureaucrat who wants to duck responsibility."[2]

Writing in the passive voice is very common among my MBA students. Apparently, the phrasing somehow feels serious and important. So pay particular attention to this, and stomp out the passive voice whenever you can. As Humes notes, "Some corporate executives like the passive because it uses convoluted phrasing that they think seems more authoritative because it sounds complex. They're wrong."[3]

Personal pronouns are fine. As Sam Leith from the *Financial Times* notes, "You do not sound grander or more important by sounding impersonal. You benefit from sounding direct and personal, by speaking as 'I' or 'we' to a 'you.'"[4]

Add Support Points

Once the headline is set, you can move on to adding the support points. This is the information that backs up the headline and makes the page credible and powerful. TED's Chris Anderson explains the process: "Flesh out each point you make with real examples, stories, facts."[5]

Support points include charts, graphs, illustrations, bullet points and pictures. There is a range of material that might back up the headline in a presentation.

In most cases, you will already know what is going on the page. When storyboarding, you might have drawn a rough chart or graph, or written out a few supporting points.

Be careful to provide strong rationale. You need to provide information that justifies your point. If your headline says, "We can reduce marketing expenses by 8 percent," you should have some rather compelling data points supporting the case.

Unsupported statements are a danger spot in a presentation; it is an area where your audience will challenge you, perhaps successfully. You need analysis to support your case.

If you can't fully support a headline, you may need to rephrase it. Generally speaking, descriptive statements are less controversial than conclusion statements and require less support. Saying "The West Region makes up most of our sales" is easy to support. You can simply show a chart with this information. Saying "We should focus on the West" is a more difficult statement because you are making a recommendation.

Sometimes you will find that a particular headline requires significant justification. You might need several charts and a long list of support points. This is a problem; you can only put a certain amount of information on each page. You need to provide the rationale, and you need clear, uncluttered pages. The solution may be that you need to rework the flow of the presentation entirely, perhaps splitting one page into two or three.

For example, the headline "Our advertising focus needs to be on urban professionals in the southern cities" may be a difficult one to support, because you are making two fairly different points, targeting urban professionals and focusing on southern cities. You would be well served to split the headline into two different pages; on the first page, you discuss the target of urban professionals, fully supporting this point, and on the second page, you discuss the importance of southern cities.

Another way to address a weak page is to soften the headline. Instead of saying "Our sales are down due to the recent warm weather," you could say, "Our sales may be suffering due to the recent warm weather." A slight wording shift puts you in a different position. You aren't stating certainty; you are just suggesting there may be a link.

Remember that your audience is not your friend and not your mother. Your audience is likely a colleague who is facing all sorts of issues and challenges, just like you are. In many cases, your audience will be your boss, or your boss's boss. They will be looking for you to deliver a strong piece of work, and will be quick to notice lapses. There is no guarantee they will support your recommendation. Sometimes they will challenge your conclusions and try to pick apart your argument. You won't necessarily get the benefit of the doubt.

Strong support is critical. Each page should have data supporting your headline. You have to answer the question: Why do you really think this headline is correct?

Some things to remember when inserting support points include the following:

DON'T HAVE MORE THAN FOUR BULLET POINTS

Nothing will kill a presentation faster than a long list of bullet points. Putting twelve or fifteen points on a page is always a problem. Nobody wants to walk through a long list of bullets. Don't do this!

There are three problems with a long list of support points. First, if you have ten or twelve points, the presentation will lose momentum. It takes a long time to review that many points. People will tend to tune out. Any forward progress that you've built in your presentation will dissipate as you wade through this long list of items.

Second, with a long list, the important points may get lost. If you have twelve support points for a specific conclusion, some are naturally going to be more significant than others. If you list them all together, the important ones may blend in; they fail to stand out and get lost.

Third, people can't remember the information. The more you tell people, the less people remember. This fact was brought to life vividly in a study done by pharmaceutical giant Eli Lilly on side effects in drug advertisements. The company showed people three versions of the same ad, and they evaluated retention. One version included four side effects, the next version listed eight side effects, and the final version showed twelve side effects. The results were striking: the more side effects in an ad, the fewer people remembered. With four side effects, people remembered an average of 1.04. With twelve side effects, retention fell to an average of only 0.85, a notable decline. As the list expanded, more and more people forgot everything on the list.[6]

The best number of bullet points is three or four. Never, ever have twelve. Please take this vow: "I promise to never put twelve or more bullet points on a page." Repeat that phrase three times.

HAVE MORE THAN ONE BULLET POINT

While having too many bullet points is a problem, having too few is also a problem. The reason is simple. Bullet points are a way of presenting a list. You can't have a list with just one thing; that isn't a list, it is just a thing. Even two bullet points seems like a fairly feeble display. Just two things? Really?

If you have just one bullet point, you probably don't need the bullet point at all. If it is one thing, perhaps your bullet point should be your headline. If you have two bullet points, perhaps you should have two pages, with each bullet being its own headline.

VARY THE VISUALS

To keep your presentation interesting, you want to change the way you present data.

Bullet points are lovely but if every page is full of bullet points, the presentation will seem dull and repetitive. Your audience will likely think, "Oh, great! Another page of bullet points. That looks a lot like the last three pages we reviewed."

Similarly, if every slide has a bar chart or a pie chart, then the presentation will appear flat. It will lack energy and excitement.

By varying the type of visual presentation, you keep it interesting. One page might have a bar chart, another page might have three bullet points and another page might have a line chart, followed by a scatter plot.

Remember, you want your audience to pay attention; you are presenting for a reason. You have a job to do. If you are asking for approval to launch your new product and your audience zones out, it is your problem, not theirs. A good way to keep your audience engaged is to make the presentation interesting.

USE SIMPLE WORDS

Many people believe that long words make you seem smarter and more credible. If I know all these big words, the logic goes, then I must be a very bright and intelligent person. As a result, my recommendation is strong.

In reality, long words have the opposite effect; using big words makes you seem less intelligent and credible. That may be the case because people think you are deliberately using big words to cover your fundamental lack of smarts (see Chapter 18 for more on the power of simple words).

PRUNE UNNECESSARY INFORMATION

If you don't really need a particular piece of information, drop it. Every figure, calculation and fact in the presentation should be there for a reason. As advertising executive Bob Rehak notes, "Fewer words mean more readers. Fewer distractions mean greater impact. Brevity enforces clarity. Clarity improves comprehension." [7]

Steve Jobs was legendary for pruning information out of a presentation. As Carmine Gallo writes in his book *The Presentation Secrets of Steve Jobs*, "Where most presenters add as many words as possible to a slide, Jobs removes and removes and removes." [8]

The Gettysburg Address, one of the most famous presentations of all time, highlights the power of pruning. President Abraham Lincoln is celebrated for what he said. What is striking is what he didn't say. He didn't discuss the details of the Battle of Gettysburg: the number of injured soldiers, the length of the battle or the scale of the conflict. He didn't mention anyone in particular, the generals or the foot soldiers. He didn't provide any background on the events leading up to the battle. He cut all the unnecessary information so that his core message came through.

Each page in a presentation should contain just enough information to support the headline. A cluttered page full of numbers does more harm than good; it will confuse and distract your audience. A better approach is to have a simple chart, graph, or series of bullet points that makes the case. Exhibit 8-1, for example, is a clear and effective page.

Exhibit 8-1

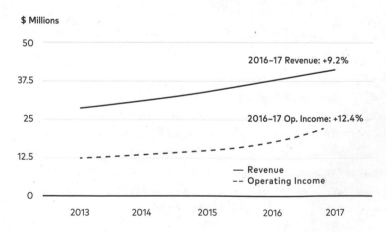

2017 WAS ANOTHER STRONG YEAR, WITH
GROWTH IN BOTH REVENUE AND PROFIT

Exhibit 8-2, from a recent PepsiCo presentation, is very different.[10] The headline states the point, and the data on the page supports it. This page is clear and easy to follow. It is a much better model.

CONSIDER PROPS

Sometimes the best way to support a point is with a prop. Steve Jobs, for example, famously used a three-legged stool at the 2008 Apple Worldwide Developers Conference to illustrate the company's businesses: Macintosh, music and the iPhone.

Props can capture people's attention and make a presentation memorable. I learned this when I washed that chicken. When you hold up a stool, people pay attention. Why is he holding up a stool? It is a welcome change from a series of slides with headlines and support points. "When you incorporate the senses—speaking of colors, sounds, smells, tastes, and textures—you engage the audience's imagination. Numbers and data rarely stick, but the language of the senses creates internal worlds and experiences that are impossible to forget," explains Gifford Booth, CEO of the TAI Group.[11]

A prop can also bring a concept to life. Productivity expert Stephen Covey, author of *The 7 Habits of Highly Effective People*, used rocks and sand to dramatize the importance of focusing on big priorities. The idea seems simple and dull when you simply say, "You should focus on the big priorities." When Covey brought out the rocks and sand, the concept came to life. It was magical. If you haven't seen it, google "Covey and rocks" and you can easily locate a video.

You should use props selectively. If you use too many, your presentation can seem a bit like a circus. As always, think about your audience and what will work best. A serious, somber CEO might not respond well to a puppet and a lollipop.

Be careful not to overwhelm the message. The goal is to sell a recommendation, not win an award for "Best Dramatic

Performance in a New Product Update Presentation." As Geoffrey James notes in his book *Business Without the Bullshit*, "You want your audience to remember your message, not how many special effects you used."[12]

Polish the Pages

Once you have the headlines and the data, you then need to polish the pages. This is the process of making your presentation look cohesive and put together. "Make it simple. Make it memorable. Make it inviting to look at. Make it fun to read," advised ad legend Leo Burnett.[13]

The difference between a polished presentation and a rough one is significant. A polished presentation simply works; it is impressive and smooth. A rough presentation looks like what it is: unfinished. "If your presentation and leave-behinds look professional, your entire organization looks professional," notes Bob Rehak.[14]

Steve Jobs understood the power of a polished presentation. According to Carmine Gallo, Jobs was "relentlessly focused on improvement, laboring over every slide, every demo, and every detail of a presentation."[15]

ANIMATIONS AND GRAPHICS

A certain amount of animation can help a presentation. Having a list of points fly in can spice up a dull list. A video clip can make a point with particular impact.

At the same time, be careful not to overproduce your presentation. The goal is to make it look professional and well done, but not to make it look like a game show. Too many whizbang special effects can be distracting, and can even suggest that you are trying to compensate for a fundamentally weak story. Each special effect is also a risk; it might not work when needed, and this will make you look unprepared.

When using graphics, be sensitive to the tone. If you are talking about laying off hundreds of salespeople, you should stay away from bright and funny graphics. If you are reviewing a big innovation, you should avoid somber pages. A presentation about the holiday party should have a very different look and feel than an update on realigning the global supply chain.

The challenge is balance. A page of black type is not going to attract a lot of attention. It looks dull. On the other hand, a page full of cartoons is exciting but often too much. Making every letter in a sentence a different color is interesting and flashy. It is also childish and distracting.

SPELLING AND GRAMMAR

Spelling and grammar matter, so spend the time to check things. Using proper grammar makes you look smart, polished and credible. A very strong presentation can lose a lot of credibility if there are grammatical mistakes throughout. "If your work is sloppily punctuated, misspelled or grammatically awry, your reader will think you have not done them the courtesy of making the effort," observes Sam Leith from the *Financial Times*.[16]

Polish, on the other hand, builds credibility. As Steven Pinker notes, "If readers can see that a writer cares about consistency and accuracy in her prose, they will be reassured that the writer cares about those virtues in conduct they cannot see so easily."[17]

Good grammar is also important for clarity. Consider these somewhat unfortunate statements:

Rachael Ray finds inspiration in cooking her family and her dog
Man eating piranha mistakenly sold as pet fish
A faculty panel on sex in college with four professors[18]

You might find it useful to send your presentation to an editor to catch mistakes; for a very small amount of money, you will significantly reduce the number of errors in your work.

FORMATTING

Perhaps the dullest part of creating a presentation is getting the formatting right. Adjusting the font and type size isn't a particularly dynamic process. It is a little methodical.

Still, formatting is important. The small details can have a surprisingly big impact on the overall presentation.

People have different preferences when it comes to formatting. Some people like one font while others support a different font. One of my colleagues at Kellogg believes Arial is the ideal font for a presentation. Another consistently uses Calibri. Some people believe the text in a presentation should always be 16 point. Others have a different opinion.

Two things are important when formatting a presentation. The first is consistency. In general, there should be a basic look and feel that carries through the document. The presentation should use just one font, with a consistent type size for headlines and support points. The simplest way to make a presentation look sloppy and unfinished is to use different fonts and sizes throughout, giving each page a different look.

At times you may want to break the format in a bid to stand out. This is fine, if done on a limited basis. Just be clear and deliberate when you are breaking away from the otherwise consistent presentation.

The second thing to remember when formatting is legibility. Ultimately, people have to be able to read the presentation. Whatever font you settle on should be easy to process. For this reason, you will generally want to avoid very flowery, elaborate fonts (see Chapter 18 for more on the impact of legibility).

Stay away from fonts like this.

Steer clear of fonts like this.

And avoid this font at all costs.

You also want to avoid small type;
it just makes it difficult for your readers.

TWO CONSIDERATIONS

You should think about two things when putting in the finishing touches. First, consider your audience. If you are presenting to someone who loves special effects, then add special effects. If they don't, then keep it simple. I once had a boss who hated animated lists; he wanted to see the complete page all at once. When presenting to him, I of course showed the full list. I cut the animations.

If you aren't sure what your boss likes, look at one of their presentations. You can generally assume they are trying to create a good presentation, so you can just copy their approach when it comes to formatting and structure.

Second, you should think about your personal brand. What does your brand stand for today? What do you want it to stand for? Your presentation should reflect your goal.

If you want your brand to be associated with analytical rigor and strategic thinking, then your presentation should generally reflect this. Stick to charts and graphs. Avoid the cartoons. Follow the template. Skip the funny cat videos.

If your goal is a personal brand strong in creativity, innovation and fresh thinking, then you should take a very different approach. Add funny graphics. Don't consistently follow the template. Limit the charts. Make some jokes.

Remember that consistency is important; you can evolve your brand but you can't change it overnight. If someone known for being analytical shows up with a goofy presentation full of Pokémon jokes, people will wonder what happened. They might think, "Is everything okay with Bill?" or "Wow! This is unexpected.

I wonder what is behind this shift?" or "Did Bill's intern create this presentation?" None of this is positive.

Writing as a Group

Creating a good presentation on your own is a challenge; it is difficult to find a compelling story and lay it out in a logical fashion.

Creating a good presentation with a team is an entirely different matter; it can be far more difficult and challenging when there are several people involved. In my experience, groups produce some of the most painful presentations.

The challenge is to capture the power of a group—creativity, insight, energy—without letting the pitfalls of group dynamics drag down the final product. You have to be particularly careful and deliberate when working with a team on a presentation.

THE WRONG APPROACH

Let's review how *not* to create a good presentation as a group.

- Determine a rough outline for the presentation.
- Divide up the different sections. Give one person the first section, another person the second section and another person the third section.
- Ask everyone to create their portion of the presentation and send the pages back by a certain date.
- Arrange the contributions in order, following the outline. Put agenda pages between each section and put a cover page on the front.
- Have each person present their section.

This approach seems logical. It divides up the work. It gets everybody involved in the action. It is likely to result in an actual document.

But it is a recipe for disaster; odds are very good that this presentation will simply not go well. This approach has many, many issues.

The first problem is the likely lack of consistency. People write differently. Some people like long headlines while others like short headlines. Some people like to end a headline with a period while others like to skip the punctuation. If you simply combine different people's slides, you will have a presentation that looks like a hodgepodge. It will be anything but the polished, smooth presentation you are striving for.

The second issue is the potential for flawed logic. This is actually a greater concern. Remember that a good presentation should tell a story. There will be a logical flow to it, with each page building from the previous page and setting up the next. It should be tight, with key concerns introduced in one section being addressed in another section.

If different people are writing different parts of the presentation, it is difficult to establish this tight connection. The overall story weakens. A point in the first section might have nothing to do with the second section. Or a recommendation in the second section may address a problem that should have been mentioned in the first section.

The third problem is one of density. One of the things we know is that people hate giving anything up. Ownership is a human emotion; we are all possessive people. Loss is also a human feeling. This means that people don't want to abandon their material. If someone creates slides, they will want to use them, whether or not the material particularly supports and connects with the overall argument.

If you ask people to go create some pages, they will likely do exactly what you asked them to do. The problem is that then they will want to see those pages in the finished document, and the presentation might then be too long, too wordy and too clunky.

Fixing these problems isn't easy. In many cases, the only way to do it is to rewrite pages and cut material. Sometimes, the presentation requires a major overhaul. This reworking process can create bad feelings on the team. Rewriting someone's headlines doesn't make them feel validated. Eliminating pages can create hard feelings and conflict. People might ask, "Why are you cutting my pages? That was important material. Who made you king of this committee? You have even more pages than I do; I think we should be cutting some of your pages. Back off!"

For this reason, group presentations are all too often very weak.

A BETTER APPROACH

In many organizations, teams are a fact of life. You don't work alone; you are part of a group. The challenge is to create a strong presentation while at the same time keeping the team engaged and connected.

One thing that doesn't work is simply excluding people from the process. It can be tempting to say, "Oh, I can take care of this presentation. Just leave it to me." You then write it and present it, easy enough. But this won't work well; you need people to be on board. If you show up with a finished product, they will likely find faults. People, especially people on a team, don't want to be left out.

The best way to get people on board is work together to create the presentation. If someone contributed to the process, they will likely support the final product. It is very hard to attack a presentation you worked on.

The challenge with a group presentation is this: you need people to be involved in the writing process, but you can't let them drive the writing process. It is a delicate balance.

The first and most important step is to agree on the recommendation. If the team isn't aligned, it will be hard or impossible to create a strong presentation. Starting to write without agreement on the core message won't work well; you will end up with pages that don't fit together.

At times, it is impossible to reach complete agreement on a recommendation; people may well have different points of view. There are ways to deal with this problem.

It is important to note that recommendations don't have to be unanimous, as on a jury. I was recently on a jury with eleven other people. We heard a rather complicated case involving a car crash and a back injury. After hearing all the testimony, we were sent to the jury room with instructions not to emerge until we had a unanimous decision. It was an exciting time; at one point eleven people agreed on a decision but one did not. The job wasn't done. We continued debating and discussing. Eventually there were ten in favor and two opposed. Things were not looking good. It was only after more discussion and compromise that we finally reached an agreement that everyone was satisfied with and had a unanimous decision.

Companies aren't like this. People can have different points of view. It is fairly unlikely that everyone on a team will agree on a particular recommendation, given the variety of backgrounds and perspectives people bring to the group. If you can't reach agreement, you can still create an effective presentation.

One option is to present both sides of the story, and then the group's recommendation. Another option is to evaluate the size of the opposition; do most people on a team support the recommendation? This logically leads to a voting situation.

Once you have agreement on the recommendation, the group can then work on crafting the story.

It is quite possible to storyboard a presentation with a group. With a whiteboard and a pen, you can sketch out a story and then seek agreement. People will likely have suggestions, which is good; they may have identified issues. At the very least, they will have input on the presentation, which should build longer-term agreement.

Once the story is clear, then people can take specific pages to collect the data and do the necessary analysis. This is sometimes a useful way to divide up the work.

When you are splitting up the analysis, don't ask people to create slides. Ask them to just gather the information and perhaps create a chart or graph. This limits the damage that pride of ownership can cause. People may not feel so connected to a particular chart. If you want to include the information, you easily can.

Remember that someone ultimately has to be responsible for the finished product. There has to be just one person who will draft the headlines. Once everyone contributes their material, one person has to take the role of polisher. This is the job of making sure one headline flows to the next, charts are formatted in a similar way and the overall presentation hangs together.

The person assembling the final version does not have to be the person who will ultimately deliver the presentation. These are two different steps: creating the presentation and delivering it.

A well-crafted presentation is easy to deliver. It is clear and logical. The data is well supported. With a good presentation, the delivery isn't all that challenging; the argument will unfold simply by going from page to page. It doesn't really matter who presents it.

There needs to be a final review step in the process, where everyone has a chance to look at and comment on the presentation. This will ensure there is alignment. It is critical at this point to check that everyone is still on board; dissension in the ranks is a huge problem.

Setting expectations is key. If people think that their slides and material will go directly into the presentation, they will be disappointed and perhaps angry when this doesn't happen. If people know right up front that things will be combined and moved around, they won't be surprised when this happens.

9

USE COMPELLING DATA

A GREAT PRESENTATION is grounded in data and information. In a business setting, people generally aren't interested in your hunch or inclination; they are looking for a recommendation that is supported by facts. As Ricardo Marques, vice president of marketing for Budweiser, observes, "Facts first, and then we make the call."[1]

You need to include compelling information in your presentation to make it credible. This is easier said than done. Some data points are stronger than others, and some presentation techniques are more powerful than others.

Focus on the Data

At some point in life, people understand that their opinion simply doesn't matter very much.

This can be a difficult moment. As children, we are encouraged to share our opinions. People praise our presentations. Teachers greet papers with positive feedback and good grades. Even a relatively poor assignment usually receives some encouraging words, with a few gentle suggestions on areas for improvement. Friends and distant acquaintances on social media respond to almost every comment with a flurry of likes and shares. At college, even the strangest views are regarded as valid and important, the reflection of individuality expressed in an open and welcoming culture.

Eventually, however, things change and we learn that our opinion simply isn't important. People don't care. When a new employee, just out of college, suggests a company make a major strategic shift, senior executives are quick to roll their eyes and dismiss it. The newcomer has no experience or expertise. Youthful enthusiasm is nice, but it often borders on naivety.

For me, this moment came early in my consulting career at Booz Allen when I was working on a sales force analysis for a major insurance company. I was looking at why some agents were far more productive than other agents. After studying the sales data for several weeks, I had a good sense of the core dynamics. I presented my thoughts to my manager. She was not impressed or moved. She simply said, "I need to see the data." My opinions were only as solid as the information backing them up.

This isn't just a factor for junior people; senior executives, even CEOs, face the same situation. A CEO may have a friendly board, quick to agree with everything presented, but there are still investors and analysts. These people don't care about opinions; they need to see the information. As Bernardo Hees, CEO of Kraft Heinz, observed in a recent presentation, "I don't think anything. Show me the data."[2]

Facts are the foundation of a great presentation. If the information is solid and strong, the presentation will hold up, just like a building constructed on solid ground. Advertising legend Leo Burnett explains, "If you have the facts on your side and honest conviction in your heart, you rarely lose by fighting for your idea all the way."[3]

If the facts are weak and unstable, the presentation can easily fall apart, much like a building built on sand. Chris Anderson from TED observes, "Style without substance is awful."[4]

As you assemble a presentation, then, it is critical to incorporate strong, solid pieces of information.

Three Types of Information

Not all information is created equal; some quotes and figures help your case substantially. Other figures are weak and easily questioned, providing little value. Some information hurts your argument and credibility.

You can put support points into three buckets: strong, irrelevant and dangerous.

STRONG SUPPORT POINTS

The core of a strong recommendation is solid support points. These facts are rock solid. They provide a stable base.

For a point to work well, it has to be clear and credible. Consider these two quotes.

Rule No.1: Never lose money. Rule No. 2: Never forget rule No.1.
WARREN BUFFETT

A satisfied customer is the best business strategy of all.
MICHAEL LEBOEUF

The first quote is from a recognizable character. Most people in business know Warren Buffett and respect his opinion. He is known as a savvy and honest business leader.

The second quote is from a relatively unknown person. Who is this, anyway? Most people won't know him, and as a result, the quote has less impact. It does little to support your case.

IRRELEVANT POINTS

The world is full of information and most of it is irrelevant to your presentation. It simply has no significance. If you are doing a presentation on pricing of a particular surgical procedure, these facts will probably have little bearing on your recommendation:

* The price of WTI crude oil in 2016 averaged $43.33 a barrel.
* It is 1,116 kilometers from Hong Kong to Manila.
* The first VCR was sold in October 1976.
* There are 7.6 million dogs in France.

You want to cut irrelevant points from your presentation; you need to identify the information that doesn't matter and then prune it.

Irrelevant data creates two problems. First, it might distract your audience. If you mention the number of dogs in France, someone might then comment, "Wow! I had no idea there were so many dogs in France. More than seven million. That is a lot of dogs! I just got a dog last year. A lot of work, dogs, but such fun. Susan, have you gotten a dog yet? I know you were thinking about it. You really should." This isn't ideal.

Second, irrelevant information obscures the information that really matters. A key analysis can easily get lost when surrounded by seven other interesting points. You want to get people to focus on the important and relevant information. This means you have to cut back everything else.

DANGEROUS POINTS

Weak support points aren't just a missed opportunity; they can be a significant problem because they can undermine your credibility.

Consider this scenario. You are presenting a recommendation to restructure pricing. It is a controversial idea; while there are reasons to support the move, there is also a risk that incremental sales won't offset the cost of the move.

In the middle of your presentation, the senior director reviewing your presentation notices that your pricing figure for a competitor is incorrect; instead of $1,546, you have $1,645. It is a small typo. You note that you flipped the numbers, a little and innocent mistake.

Unfortunately, this small mistake creates a big problem. The executive now looks at all the other figures in the presentation, searching for mistakes. They also start to wonder if there are other errors in the analysis. If you flipped the revenue figure, then you might have flipped a pricing figure. If you flipped a pricing figure, then perhaps the entire analysis is flawed. You can't make a big decision on a flawed analysis.

At the end of the meeting they note, "Well, this has been an interesting discussion but clearly we need to think more about it." They head off. The meeting was a failure; it did not convince the target. Instead, it raised doubts and questions. It did more harm than good.

If someone can identify a problem with your data, they then have a reason to question your entire recommendation. Small mistakes can create big problems.

Facts and Belief

There is a difference between information that is true and information that is believable. Just because something is true doesn't mean that it is believable. People don't believe everything that is true, and sometimes they believe things that are false.

For many years people debated about whether the Earth was flat or round. Those favoring the round point of view were correct, but they were not able to convince others.

In a presentation, it is best to base your recommendation on things that are both true and believable. These facts and figures will strengthen your case substantially; people will grasp the information, believe it and see how it connects to your recommendation.

If you present a rather surprising finding from a particular analysis, people may not believe it. They might think

- you are using incorrect information,
- you did the wrong calculation or
- you made a mathematical mistake.

If someone questions your figures, if they don't believe your findings, you can have a significant problem. They may quickly dismiss the analysis and, as a result, question the entire report.

Remember this when assembling your argument. For each fact, consider whether your audience will believe it. Ask yourself, "Will they believe this piece of information or not?"

It you are presenting facts that people will likely believe, you are in good shape. Simply include the information. If your audience is likely to be surprised by your data, proceed with care.

The first question: Do you need to include this information? If it isn't critical, you might be better off just leaving it out. Why risk it? If the data plays an important part in your analysis, consider building up to it. Explain the analytical approach or the source. Once people agree with the basis for the information, it will be harder for them to discard it.

You also could use allies to support the data. If a respected person endorses the information, it becomes more credible. When I was at Kraft, a piece of market research data gained more significance if the head of market research explained that the approach was viable and significant.

Stories

A presentation shouldn't be all facts and figures. Stories can be equally effective, sometimes more effective. The problem with numbers is that they lack emotion. A table just sits there. It isn't memorable. It doesn't move you.

A story, by contrast, can bring everything to life. You can show data on purchase habits of new moms, but a story about the time you spoke with a new mom is much more engaging. I teach a business case about sepsis in one of my classes at Kellogg. I can tell students that sepsis is a terrible disease, and I can show the grim statistics, but the class doesn't really sit up and engage until I tell a story about a Kellogg student who became septic while working on a consulting project in Germany, spent a month in a German hospital, unconscious, swelled up to twice his normal size, and almost didn't survive.

Stories are interesting. Kellogg professor Craig Wortmann teaches strategic selling at Kellogg and wrote the book *What's Your Story?* He explains that stories are powerful because they create engagement: "In the very act of telling a story, we can't help but engage people. The act of telling and the act of listening build the necessary engagement to help get important information and knowledge across."[5] Stories also provide a welcome break in the presentation. As Wortmann notes, "Almost unconsciously stories make us slow down and listen."[6]

As you build your case, think about stories that support your argument. You might not actually put the story in the written presentation; you might just tell it when you go through a certain section.

An effective story should have three characteristics. First, it should be brief. In a business discussion, people rarely have patience for a long, detailed narrative. Get to the point! Second, it should be true. You want to speak from the heart. It is easiest to do this if you are telling an actual story. Third, it should support the data. A story on its own wouldn't be particularly credible; you are just reporting on a single person or incident. It could be an isolated situation. Ideally, you show the data and then tell the story, or you tell the story and then show the data. This way, you are using two different approaches to make your point.

For example, this combination of fact and story is powerful: "The vast majority of MBA students view recruiting as a top priority. In our most recent study, 68 percent of our MBAs put recruiting at the top of the list. I saw this just last week; my classroom was only about half full because students were out on second-round interviews."

One important note: the best stories are your own; they are experiences from your life. These stories are authentic. In addition, you can easily remember them and respond to questions.

Simple and Complicated Analyses

When in doubt, it is best to use simple analyses. If your calculations are easy to follow, people will believe them; they can see the actual numbers.

Solid support points are comprehensible. If someone doesn't understand a figure or calculation, it won't help your argument. You aren't going to lose people when you say that 18 plus 14 equals 32. You will confuse them if you start talking about binomial distribution and Chebyshev's inequality.

Be careful about advanced analytics. A complicated set of equations might be very nifty, but if people don't understand what you are doing, it won't help your argument. Be careful, too, about using new types of information; presenting new data from the latest social media platform might seem impressive, but it won't be very powerful since people don't know what they are looking at.

A complicated set of calculations will be difficult for your audience to follow. This is a problem for two reasons. First, your audience might just skip the analysis entirely. Who wants to wade through a dense batch of numbers? It your audience skips the analysis, it adds no value. If anything, it distracts from the key points.

Second, the analysis will tax your audience's mental capacity. Daniel Kahneman, the Nobel Prize–winning psychologist, explored the idea of cognitive load in his book *Thinking, Fast and Slow*. Complex analyses and difficult charts impose a mental burden on people, making it more difficult to get agreement and commitment. If you want to persuade people, Kahneman writes, "The general principle is that anything you can do to reduce cognitive strain will help."[7]

Consider two exhibits:

Exhibit A

$$100 + 21 = 121$$

Exhibit B

The TC model shows that
the answer is 121.

THE FIRST EXHIBIT is simple. You nod your head and see the calculation. It is hard to disagree with it. The second calculation introduces a new level of complexity in the form of a model. What is the TC model? What goes into it?

In general, you will be far better off sticking with simple, easy-to-follow calculations, exhibits and data points. Use figures that people understand. Make the labeling clear. Show your work.

The simple calculations create confidence. When you present a simple calculation that people can follow, you aren't asking them to trust you; you are simply showing them the numbers and the data. It is clear and logical.

Still, there are rare times when you may need to use a complex analysis. It could be that you really need the set of calculations to show a key point. A heavy dose of analytics also can increase your credibility.

If you are using a complex analysis in a presentation, you need to explain it before you actually incorporate the information. Prior to presenting the results of a purchase multivariate regression model analysis, you should first show how a purchase multivariate regression model works. Then you can review your inputs. Only then should you show the results of the analysis and discuss the implications.

Understand the Data

It is important to know what each piece of information means; you have to understand your data.

You might think that this is a simple task. It is not. Even a simple piece of data can create quite a bit of complexity. What precisely is the information?

Take something as basic as market share. You might see that you have a market share of 18.7 percent. This is an interesting fact, and it might be an important thing to include in your presentation.

Before you use the figure, however, you should think about it. What is that figure, anyway?

The first set of questions: What is the time frame? Is that for this week, this month or this year? Is it YTD or the last fifty-two weeks?

The next set of questions: What is the base? Is that share for all retail outlets? Or is it just for grocery stores? What geography does it cover?

And then, what type of share is it, anyway? Is the figure showing a percentage of unit sales or a percentage of dollar sales?

Furthermore, what is included in that share figure? Does it reflect the core business, or does it include all the recent new products?

Understanding your data is key. If someone asks about a figure, you want to reply quickly and confidently. The only way to do this is to consider the information in depth before you present it.

Not knowing your information is dangerous. When someone asks, "So, Aviv, is that a dollar-share figure or unit-share figure?"

you don't want to respond "I don't know" or "Let me check" or, even worse, "What is the difference?" This does not help your credibility.

Sources

For a presentation to be credible, you need to know where each piece of information comes from and what it means. The sources should be strong, so the data is not up for debate.

USE CREDIBLE SOURCES

Some sources are more reliable and credible than others. To a large degree this is a question of trust. You want your audience to trust the information. One way to do this is to rely on proven sources. Many people trust leading news organizations like the *Financial Times* and the *New York Times*. People also trust academic journals, such as the *New England Journal of Medicine* and the *Journal of Marketing*.

Inside a company, some sources and reports are likely more studied and trusted than others. When I worked at Kraft Foods, for example, people trusted the weekly sales data that we received from Nielsen. If you referred to this information, people would not raise questions about it. People were more skeptical of the analysis and data provided by mix model firm Rak & Company. If you used information from one of the reports from Rak & Company, people were quick to raise questions.

Consider these three statements:

- The average new car now sells for $28,457.
- Bob on the loading dock said the average new car now sells for $28,457.
- Cars.com reports that the average new car now sells for $28,457.

The first statement doesn't carry a lot of weight. Where did that figure come from? Did you just make it up? Am I simply supposed to believe what you said? If I'm a skeptical person, and many business executives are, a figure floating around like this has very little value.

The second statement has a source, which is good; you didn't make it up. Overall, however, it is even less credible; Bob on the loading dock might be a lovely person, but unless he is regarded as an expert within the company, it is unlikely he is up-to-date on the latest automotive sales figures.

Including Bob as a reference is actually a fairly damaging move. The figure has little credibility, and the simple fact that you included Bob as a reference in your presentation raises questions about your judgment. You really should know better. Your personal brand just took a hit.

The third statement is a solid, credible statement. Cars.com is a leading seller of autos, so it has access to solid data. If Cars.com says the average price is now $28,457, then the average selling price is probably $28,457.

INCLUDE THE REFERENCE

You should include the source for every piece of significant information in your presentation.

Saying there are 142,897 spectrometers in the United States is potentially a good thing. This statement will be much stronger if you point out that this data comes from a respected source like the *Wall Street Journal*.

The source information should be appropriately detailed. The key is that someone should be able to go track down the piece of information if they wanted to verify your work. If you found a quote on a website, write out the website and note when you found it. If you located a key figure in a US government report, list the report, the date and the page.

It is always a good practice to use a consistent citation format; this thorough approach makes you look rigorous. People use different citation formats in different settings, so check that you are using the correct format. One easy way to do this is to watch what your boss does when it comes to noting sources.

The source information should not be prominent; you can make the reference very small. Indeed, this is the best approach; you want to avoid cluttering the page with too much information. At the same time, the reference should be readily available for a reader.

Don't make people ask about the source; just include the reference as a matter of practice. If you force people to ask, this will slow down the presentation. More important, you don't want to devote your mental capacity to remembering source information; you should devote your capacity to remembering key analyses and particularly significant pieces of information.

Check Your Numbers

The most important thing to remember when working with data and information is that you need to check your numbers. You have to be 100 percent certain that the numbers are right, you have the source correct, the date is correct, the labeling is correct.

Remember that mistakes cause a host of problems; you want to do everything possible to avoid an error in the numbers.

Many people think of mistakes the same way they think of cockroaches. If you see one, you know there are many more lurking about.

Mistakes can also lead you to completely wrong conclusions. If you flip a couple numbers, the decision to expand into a new market may no longer make financial sense, or your pricing recommendation could look like a bad move instead of a good move.

Before finalizing a presentation, then, you should spend some time looking at all the factual data. Check each number. Review each analysis. If it looks funny, or if you can't find the source, you should check it and rework it.

Ultimately, a strong presentation needs to be grounded in solid data. Kraft Heinz's Bernardo Hees was correct when he observed, "Opinions don't matter. Facts do."[8]

10

PRESELL

THERE IS ONLY one way to guarantee that a presentation will go well: presell it. If you meet with all of the key players before a meeting, take them through the document and get them on board with the recommendation, you can be confident that things will end on a positive note.

Many meetings are largely a formality. Everyone in the room has seen the recommendation and supports it, so people nod and agree, and approve the plan.

Preselling doesn't guarantee success, of course—things can always go off the tracks—but if you spend time preselling before the meeting, then the odds will be in your favor.

Two Scenarios

Consider two different scenarios:

SCENARIO 1:
You are making a key recommendation for your business. It will involve trade-offs and tough choices. People have different

opinions about the issue. You walk in hoping the presentation will go well. Your recommendation catches people by surprise. Some warm to it immediately; some have questions. Others, needing time to ponder it, say little.

The meeting is a challenge. You have to field tough questions from the opponents. A few of these questions will catch you off guard, so you aren't ready for them. You are forced to resort to the classic fallback line: "I will get back to you later to clarify things."

The discussion concludes with no agreement. Some people are intrigued, others are opposed, and others have real concerns. Many don't know exactly what to think.

At this point, you are in a terrible position. The meeting served no purpose; you didn't get the agreement you were seeking. So you will probably have to do the meeting again. This is not the outcome you were hoping for.

Only the situation is actually worse than it seems, because now you've lost control of the discussion. People will debate the issue in separate talks and you won't be there. Someone with concerns might hunt for data supporting their position, and track down some of the undecided people and try to sway their opinions. Even your supporters may waver as they hear objections and see your inability to manage them. The entire recommendation is likely to fall apart.

SCENARIO 2:

You are making a key recommendation for your business. It will involve trade-offs and tough choices. People have different opinions about the issue. You walk in knowing where people stand. There are three people who support it and two with concerns. Everyone is familiar with the issues.

Your presentation does two things: it reinforces the opinions of the supporters, and it addresses all the concerns of the skeptics. You provide data showing you've thought through all the possible issues and the alternate plans.

The meeting ends with either agreement or a thoughtful discussion of the points of conflict. People talk about the issues and seek resolution.

You finish the meeting with a clear decision.

The difference between the two scenarios above is simple. In the first case, there was no advance work, so things went awry. In the second case, efforts before the meeting laid the groundwork for success.

It is all too easy to skip the preselling phase and just head into the presentation cold. After all, many people think, the presentation matters most, right? So let's make the presentation perfect.

In reality, failing to lay the groundwork for a presentation dramatically increases your risk. The presentation might still go well, but the risk that it won't go well is significant.

Remember, presentations can accelerate or kill you career. Why take a chance?

Why Preselling Is Important

There are several reasons why preselling is such an important part of the presenting process.

LEARN WHERE PEOPLE STAND

The first reason to presell is that you want to figure out what people think before you get into the room. Do they support your recommendation? Do they have concerns? Are they vehemently opposed?

If you know where people stand, you can adjust your approach. If you know people are on board, you can assume the meeting will go well. You can move quickly; you try to get people nodding and just keep pressing forward. You can spend much of the time on next steps, working with the group on ways to address challenges you might encounter in the future.

If you know people oppose your recommendation, however, then you will need take a very different approach. You might go more slowly, emphasizing each point as you build your case. You will need to study your audience to find the objections and then work to overcome them. You might want to talk with your supporters before the meeting, so they are ready to chime in and promote the recommendation.

On occasion, you might decide to rework the presentation entirely, going back to the writing phase. Remember that when you construct a presentation, you need to have a picture of your audience in your mind. Who are these people? What do they like? What do they know and believe? If you find out your understanding of your audience is incorrect, then the presentation might not work. Instead of delivering a recommendation forcefully, you may want to approach it in a gentler fashion, putting forth different options and assessing each one.

If things really look bad, you might cancel the meeting entirely. Why do a presentation when you know the recommendation won't be approved? In most cases, you will want to avoid the situation. It isn't a great use of time. We encounter enough conflict and rejection as it is.

IDENTIFY OBJECTIONS

Every time you take people through a presentation, you test your argument. You can see how people react and identify stumbling blocks. You can also identify objections: reasons why someone might go against the proposed plan.

Understanding concerns is critical; you want to identify reasons why your point of view might not be correct. Often we don't know the objections; if we didn't believe in the recommendation, we wouldn't be making it. Finding out that someone has questions about production capacity or sales force execution is a step forward.

Once you know the concerns, you can deal with them. You can assemble data that negates the issue and puts people at ease. Do we have production capacity? We do. Can the sales force execute the program? Absolutely.

In some cases, you will put this information in your presentation, shifting the flow a bit to make room for the data. In other situations, you might hang on to the information and simply discuss it during the presentation, or have it as a backup slide in case the question comes up.

Sometimes the objections will be both real and significant. This might force you to rethink your entire recommendation. It is easy to dismiss the concerns people bring up, but often there is validity in the points. It might be that there really isn't production capacity or there are sales force execution issues.

The key point is this: you won't know all the issues until you talk to people. So you've got to take them through the recommendation and get their assessment.

If you don't find problems, it doesn't mean they've vanished, just as not seeing cockroaches in your house doesn't mean they aren't there. Rest assured, problems, and cockroaches, will eventually turn up. Perhaps this will be during the presentation. This is not ideal. Worse, the problem will appear during the actual product launch, when your grand plan goes awry due to a problem that was present from the early days of the program.

GET IDEAS

One of the best reasons to presell a document is that you can get people's ideas. This will make your presentation stronger.

Someone might recommend that you show a particular calculation or mention a key issue. This is great feedback. Another person might suggest that you think about competitive dynamics or some other issue. This is also useful feedback. Someone might find a typo.

Your goal is to capture ideas before the presentation. If someone asks in the presell meeting, "So what is the breakeven on the digital advertising campaign?" all is well. You can do the calculation to see what it says. Then you can include it in the presentation if it adds to the argument. Or you can have it ready to go in case the question comes up. Or you can just drop in a reference to the calculation during your presentation, casually noting, "And the breakeven analysis shows that this program needs only a 4 percent lift to justify the expense."

During the actual presentation there is a very different dynamic. If someone asks about the break-even calculation and you haven't done it, you look unprepared. Why didn't you do that, anyway? Isn't it a fairly basic, core analysis?

Remember to follow up on suggestions! It is tempting to ignore certain comments. Someone might ask, "So what are sales in Ireland, anyway?" or point out a little flaw: "I think the alignment in this paragraph is off." These are little issues, so they are easy to ignore.

Don't do this. If you don't act on a suggestion, you send the signal that it either wasn't a good idea or you thought it was too trivial to matter. This doesn't win people over.

You should actually listen closely for the little ideas. These are easy ways to demonstrate to people that you heard their ideas and care about their input. When they see that you addressed their points, they will likely think that you are appreciative and responsive. They may not thank you for fixing the alignment in the paragraph, but they will notice. Don't miss the small wins.

SHOW RESPECT

Taking the time to meet with someone before a big meeting is a way to show respect. The move sends a clear message: "You are important and I care about your opinions." This is an excellent way to secure support.

The Approach

When preselling a presentation, you should schedule a series of small meetings. You might set up a meeting with the head of sales, for example, and then a meeting with the head of market research. In each meeting you begin in a similar fashion, saying, "We have a meeting coming up on Project Hamster, and I want to take you through our latest draft to get your ideas and input."

It is important to walk through a draft, not the final document. Ideally, you'll print on the cover page in large letters "DRAFT" or "WORKING DRAFT" or "INITIAL DRAFT." If you show up with the final document, it looks like you aren't really asking for their input; you are simply showing them the document, following some protocol. This is better than nothing but it misses the key point. You really do want their input and suggestions.

The presell meetings should be several days or even a week before the actual presentation. Very often people will have suggestions; they might recommend a particular analysis, or suggest that you meet with a particular person. You need some time to follow up on the ideas; if someone asks for a particular analysis, you want to have time to actually do it.

Meeting with someone just before a critical meeting is a bad idea. When they ask for changes, you won't be able to make them. If they have concerns, you will be in a difficult spot. You can press on with the meeting, but now you'll be uncertain and nervous. You will have to dance around their concerns. Alternatively, you can cancel the meeting and try to reschedule it, but this is also a bad option; scheduling meetings is not easy, and a last-minute delay suggests to everyone that there was some problem. When you finally do get around to the presentation, your audience might view things with a heightened level of skepticism.

For this reason, it is usually better to skip the presell meeting than try to fit it in just before a presentation.

When taking someone through the draft, watch closely. Do they nod their head? Do they smile? Do they furrow their brow? On a more basic level, are they interested or not? All of this information is helpful.

At this point you desperately want input. What other information would they like to see? Where are the gaps? What are the issues?

You then want to follow up. Some people take a while to think through things; you should take this into account. A simple email two days later can do the trick. Simply write, "Susan, it was great to see you on Tuesday. I wanted to follow up to see if you had any other questions about the recommendation. I would be happy to stop by to discuss it if that would be easier." If someone expressed concerns about your recommendation, a second meeting is useful to show that you heard the issues, reflected on them and then responded in some fashion.

Learning from BBQ Sauce

I saw the power of laying the proper groundwork when I restaged the Kraft BBQ Sauce business. After years of deep discounts and cost cuts, the business was in a desperate situation. Results were good but the path was unsustainable.

The solution was clear: cut the discounts, improve product quality and invest in new advertising to rebuild perceptions. This was a major shift for the business, an investment in differentiation and quality. The problem was that it was an expensive plan and profits would fall dramatically in the first two years.

The project eventually resulted in a meeting with the division president. He wanted to know the plan and the projected impact. The project would only proceed with his approval.

I got busy on the presentation. I worked with my team to tell the story, supporting key points with solid data. It was a strong case.

Once we had the rough presentation, I scheduled meetings with my cross-functional peers: all the different people who would be at the meeting. I met with the head of sales, the head of market research, the director of finance, the operations manager. In each meeting I went through the presentation, addressed each person's questions and got their suggestions. I then revised the document to reflect their input.

By the time the meeting came along, I was confident it would go well. There was only one person who hadn't seen the final presentation: the division president. Everyone else knew exactly what was coming.

The presentation went well. I explained the situation and the recommendation. Once I was done, the division president asked different cross-functional executives if they were on board. Not surprisingly, given my investment in preselling, they all were.

We moved ahead and, after a very rough year, the Kraft BBQ business started growing in the right manner, with profitable growth based on product quality and stronger brand equity.

11

PREPARE AND PRACTICE

AS THE PRESENTATION approaches, preparation and practice become critical. You have to focus on all the details to make sure things go smoothly. If you are attentive in the days leading up to the presentation, you will lay the groundwork for success.

Some people think presentations just happen. People schedule the time and show up, ready to go. This is rarely the case. A business presentation and a theater production have a lot in common when it comes to the need for preparation. Performers don't take the stage unless they know their roles very well. You don't head out with the attitude that "I really don't know what I'm supposed to do or say, but I'll give it a shot." You don't just wing it. Even improv performers have a general flow in mind when they begin; there is one activity and it will lead to the next activity.

If you're poorly prepared for a show, it isn't likely to go well. People will stumble over their lines. The timing won't quite work. People may move awkwardly around the stage. Someone might trip. You can see this if you attend a dress rehearsal. Things are a little rough. It isn't smooth and fluid. You can tell it isn't quite ready.

Presenters have the same need for preparation. You don't want to head into a presentation until you are ready. You need to know what is going to happen. A little bit of preparation can improve the production dramatically.

I recently witnessed the importance of preparation in my marketing strategy course at Kellogg when I hosted a new guest speaker. I frequently rely on guest speakers to bring fresh examples to the class and illustrate how the concepts we discuss come to life in the real world. I've learned, however, that preparation is essential for success. Someone new to the Kellogg classroom won't necessarily do a great job. It is a different environment with some unique dynamics, and Kellogg students tend to be a demanding crowd, looking for insights and learnings all along the way. So, before the class session, I had two conversations. First, I talked with the speaker. I encouraged him to interact with the class. In particularly, I urged him to call on students. One of the most powerful tools a teacher can use for getting a conversation going on any topic is the cold call. If you want to start a debate on immigration, call on someone to provide an opinion. And then call on someone else to either agree or disagree with that opinion. Before you know it, you have a lively discussion going.

This is a useful tool for a guest speaker. Tossing out a general question like "So, what do you think?" will often result in no response from a classroom full of students; the presenter will simply sit there, looking awkward. A specific question, directed to a particular person, will always result in an interesting response: "Susan, what do you think about the food at McDonalds?"

Second, I spoke with the class. I told them that when guest speakers simply talk for ninety minutes, a class session will usually drag. Few people can be engaging for that long. So the students' task was to ask lots of questions. Everyone loves answering questions. Having too many questions wasn't a problem; the presenter could always cut off the flow. The result? A terrific class session. The presenter did a tremendous job; he was energized by the activity and the questions. The students loved the class. It was interesting and informative; the speaker's engaging approach connected with the students.

Of course, it didn't just happen. I had carefully constructed the situation to maximize the odds of success. The lesson is simple: you have to prepare for a presentation. You have to spend the time to lay the groundwork and ensure that everything goes well.

Prepare

There are several key things to consider when preparing for a presentation.

PEOPLE

The most important preparation point is people. Can you get the right people to attend? If you are hoping to get a decision, you need all the key influencers to be present.

If the right people aren't there, it can be difficult to move forward. You don't want to go through a presentation and have it end up with "Well, we really need to hear from the operations team before we can make a final decision. Let's try to schedule some time with Marcia in the next couple weeks." This simply means that you have to repeat the entire presentation.

You want to think carefully about how many people you are inviting. It is tempting to include a lot of people; there are cross-functional groups that may want to be included. You may have junior people who want to see the discussion. It would be nice to include the summer intern so they can see how these meetings go.

The problem is that a large group can stifle conversation, especially if your key decision maker likes a smaller group.

When sorting out who should attend, remember your goals. You aren't doing the presentation to train or entertain people. You are trying to accomplish an objective.

SPACE

You should think about the room as you prepare for the meeting. Have you reserved the right space? Environment matters; our physical environment has a notable impact on how we feel and how we behave. Later in the book I talk about how to set up for a presentation. At this stage the focus is on securing the ideal location.

The room should be big enough but not too big. People do not want to be stuck in a cramped, tiny room. This is uncomfortable and might put people in a bad mood. If there aren't enough chairs, the first five or ten minutes of your meeting will be spent locating more seats and bringing them into the room. This is not a compelling way to use your limited time.

You don't want too big a room, either, because people might feel a little lost. Meeting with three people in an auditorium is not a best practice; you feel dwarfed, small and uncomfortable in the cavernous space.

Reserve the room for at least a half hour before your presentation. This will give you time to set up and get organized. If you reserve a room at 2 p.m. for a 2 p.m. meeting, you will be scrambling. The prior group might not finish until 2 or even 2:05. You will then need to frantically set up your materials.

CONSIDER COPIES

Should you distribute copies, or not? If you decide to give people copies, when will you do it? Will you send the presentation ahead of time or hand out copies after the actual event? These are also important questions to consider.

Of course, before a key meeting you will want to meet with key people to understand their views and take them through the key points. So, you'll have to show people part of the analysis before the actual gathering. The question is when to send out the final document.

To a large degree, the answer to this question will depend on your audience. If your CEO wants a copy in advance, you should give them a copy in advance. When I was at Booz Allen, for example, I had a manager who insisted on receiving every presentation at least two days before the meeting. So that is what I did.

I favor giving people copies just before the meeting. This way they will have the hard copy in case they want to take notes. They can bounce around the presentation if they lose the flow or want to spend a bit more time on an analysis than you provided. They don't have to worry about writing everything down; this makes them less anxious and more comfortable.

Sending a presentation a day or two before a meeting is more debatable. On the one hand, people have an opportunity to read it and think about it. Of course, they do this without your commentary; you are relying just on your written deck to carry the argument.

One problem with sending the presentation in advance is that inevitably some people will read it and others won't. This will create a bit of a tension in the meeting. People who have read the document will want to go quickly. They might not even want to go through the presentation at all; they will just want to ask questions and debate. This completely takes away your ability to talk through a story. People who haven't read the document will be lost; they will want to go through the presentation, and really can't participate in a discussion about the document because they haven't read it.

Practice!

When I talk with gifted speakers about presenting tips, one suggestion comes up again and again: practice.

People don't just get up and present in an eloquent fashion, or at least most people don't. Without practice, you might get bogged down in too many details or stories, or you might end up going too fast, skipping over key points. You might end up providing examples that don't quite work or, even worse, examples that don't support your point.

Great speakers practice. Winston Churchill prepared intensely for every address, practicing six to eight hours before a forty-minute talk. So did Steve Jobs. "Here's his presentation secret," writes author Carmine Gallo. "Jobs rehearses for hours. To be more precise, many, many hours over many, many days." [1]

Do a few things to get the most out of your practice time.

WALK THROUGH THE SLIDES

When practicing, you want to walk through your slides, page by page, and consider the points you will make. The goal is not to memorize your talk. This will rarely go well; you will become stressed trying to remember it and it won't feel natural. The objective is to know the presentation, so you can tell the story.

It is important to actually deliver the presentation; you can't just think about it. What will you say for each page? "The *only* way to prepare a presentation is to speak it aloud, just as you will on the day of your actual presentation," recommends presentation coach Jerry Weissman. [2]

You also want to gesture. What will you physically do as you present each page? Will you point at a particular figure? Will you spend time explaining a calculation?

One way to do this is to simply stand up in your office and walk through it, talking to a lamp or a potted plant.

Another option is to present to colleagues. You gather several peers in a room and go through the slides. This can feel awkward but it is a very effective approach.

Videotaping yourself is yet another good approach. You set up a recording device and deliver the presentation. Then you go back and watch it, observing and critiquing how you appear. This is a painful process but it can be very effective. Personal branding expert Brenda Bence observes, "Watching yourself can be a tremendous eye-opener. It may not be something you enjoy, but it will almost certainly show you what you need to work on in order to improve the way you're perceived."[3]

IDENTIFY TALKING POINTS

As you go through the presentation, you should focus on identifying the talking points. Is there an interesting story that supports your point? Is there information on the slides that is particularly important?

You may find it useful to write notes on each page. You don't want to write out detailed comments; you won't be able to read these in any event. But it might be useful to note, "Tell story about Columbian business here," or "Ask if people saw last year's net promoter score results."

It is important to consider each section. Will a particular story enhance your argument or not? As Carmine Gallo recommends, "Practice, practice and practice some more. Don't take anything for granted. Review every slide, every demo, and every key message."[4]

By the time you are done, you should know your presentation exceptionally well. You should know each page and each talking point. With this level of preparation, you won't need much in the way of notes.

FOCUS ON TIMING

Managing your time is a key challenge. You want to spend time on the important pages, not on the unimportant pages. If you have some wonderful stories related to points that are not significant, your best move is to drop them. This can be painful; we all love telling a great story. Still, spending scarce time on a point that doesn't really matter is not a good idea.

In general, you should plan to finish early. If your presentation is scheduled to run from 10 to 11:30, you should shoot for finishing up by 11:15. With this type of planning, everything will work out well. If you actually finish at 11:15, people will be happy to have some bonus time to check emails, locate a cup of coffee or make a phone call. You rarely get in trouble for finishing a meeting too early. If you get a lot of questions, you have some time to work with; you can pause to fully respond to the inquiries.

Trying to fit too much stuff into a presentation is never a good idea. If you plan to use all of your time, even a simple question can delay you. Then at the end of the meeting, you have a series of bad options.

Option 1: You can rush through pages in a desperate bid to finish up. This doesn't go well. You start speaking quickly and racing through the material.

Option 2: You can cut people off, saying, "John, I love your involvement but I've really got to keep moving." This is even worse, because now you are shutting down John. This doesn't make John feel good. Remember, your goal is to get approval for your recommendation, so you need people on board.

Option 3: You could address the questions and never finish the presentation. This is a terrible option; you then can decide to return sometime to finish it, which isn't likely to happen, or you can count on people reading it back in their office, which they simply won't do. At the end of the meeting, you want to leave time for the group to reach agreement, or at least to review the next steps so everyone knows what happens going forward.

So, managing the time is critical, and you have to leave more rather than less.

The problem is that you can't entirely control the flow of a meeting. Someone might have a series of questions, and answering these takes time. The vice president might get into a side conversation on travel plans, which consumes your meeting time.

It all can be frustrating. In the middle of a meeting on pricing, someone might say, "Hey, Susan, did we ever hear back from Carrefour about that in-store seasonal promotion idea?"

Susan responds, "Well, Dave, we did. But they said the week of October 9th wasn't available, so they asked if we could move the promotion to the following week."

And the conversation then unfolds. "Miguel, could the sales team execute that week?"

"That would really be a problem, Dave, because we have the national sales meetings exactly at that moment."

"Susan, can we ask Carrefour about early November? That might be a better time," says Dave.

And Susan responds, "I can ask. I think that is a pretty soft week for the category, however. Sam, can you check on that?"

While this lively discussion takes place, you are standing in front of the room, looking awkward and wondering how you will get through your presentation.

Time is one reason why the executive summary is such an important part of a presentation. You want to establish your key points early in the meeting, so if things don't go smoothly, you don't leave the meeting without ever having gotten to your main points. The executive summary is your disaster plan.

BE READY TO REVISE

We like to think of things proceeding in a logical fashion, step-by-step, marching forward toward a goal. This is sometimes how things work out with a presentation; the writing comes before the practicing, which in turn comes before the actual event.

Many times, however, things are not quite so orderly; the entire process spirals around. We find ourselves going backward, revisiting prior steps.

Practicing a presentation will often reveal problems. It may be that a page lacks supporting data. Why should someone believe your statement? It isn't clear. Other times the flow isn't quite right; the sequence of pages is awkward. There is a natural question but the presentation doesn't address it.

If this is the case, go back and revise the presentation. Change the flow if need be, add more data or change the structure.

This is one reason why it is difficult to create a brilliant presentation at the last minute. If you begin rehearsing the evening before a key meeting, there is little time to revise things. If you've sent out copies, you are locked into the flow.

CONSIDER GETTING A COACH

If you've struggled with presentations, you may find it useful to hire a communications coach, someone who can give you tips and suggestions.

A coach is valuable because they will generally know about presenting, and will be willing to provide honest feedback. Friends and colleagues may not give you real feedback. It can be difficult to tell someone they say "you know" or "um" after every sentence.

Hiring a coach is both emotionally challenging and expensive. Still, given the importance of presenting, it can be an excellent financial investment. Legendary investor Warren Buffett overcame his deep fear of public speaking by taking a course at Dale Carnegie. He explains, "If I hadn't of done that, my whole life would have been different."[5] Jim Kilts, CEO of companies such as Kraft Foods, Nabisco and Gillette, struggled with presenting and worked with a coach. He observes, "While speech training doesn't rank on a level with physical torture in terms of pain and suffering, it certainly exacts a toll—especially on your psyche and identity."[6]

12

SET THE ROOM

SEVERAL YEARS AGO I had the opportunity to watch one of my colleagues at Kellogg teach a course on the health-care industry. It was a highly informative class and I learned a lot; he is an expert in his field and a very skilled teacher.

I was struck, however, by how this professor arrived for the class sessions. For a class that started at 6 p.m., he would consistently walk into the room at 5:58, his hands full of copies and notes. He would then scramble to get ready; he would open up his computer, turn on the projector and organize all his materials. Most days, not surprisingly, something didn't work properly; the projector was on the blink or he couldn't get the sound connection operating. So, he raced around attempting to set things straight. He looked very stressed and concerned.

To his credit, most days he was able to start the class more or less on time. He wasn't precisely on the dot but it was close enough that students didn't seem to mind. Still, on some evenings the snafus were such that the class started ten or fifteen minutes late.

The chaotic start didn't set the class up for success. He began the class session stressed and harassed, so the first few minutes were anything but smooth. After a while, he relaxed and his energy level fell. For students, the start sent all the wrong messages. First, there was anxiety; when the professor is scrambling, students sense it. Then there was a fall in energy, as the class picked up on his relief and relaxation.

You want a class to start with positive energy and anticipation, perhaps even excitement. The pre-class scramble set the opposite tone.

Recently I watched a different speaker prepare for a class. He arrived very early and set up his materials. He checked the computer and sound, and laid out his notes. Then, for the ten minutes leading up to the talk, he simply walked around and talked with students. He asked where they were from and what sort of work they did. He asked what they hoped to learn from the session.

It was casual and light conversation, but it sent some important messages. First, the approach communicated that the speaker was confident and in control; this session would go well. Second, it sent the message that the speaker cared about the participants. This all set the class up for success.

Perhaps the single easiest thing you can do to ensure your presentation will go well is to arrive early and get ready for the event. You want to organize the room.

Setting the room is important for several reasons. The most important one is simple: you can find and address technical issues. There will usually be some problems. Technology isn't perfect. If you get to the room with little time to spare, you will have to scramble when the inevitable problems arise. If you get there early, you can fix things or figure out an alternate plan.

Getting to the room early will also put you at ease. When you know everything is all set, you will be comfortable. This will settle you down. Presenting is a stressful activity. Technical problems only increase the stress level. If you have time, you won't be running around in a concerned state. You can take a deep breath, flip through your notes, chat with participants or refill your coffee.

To set the room, you should do several things.

Arrive Early

The most important thing is to get to the meeting well ahead of time. For casual presentations at the office, this might be twenty minutes. For a major event, you'll want to leave more time, perhaps even an hour or more.

Presenting can be stressful. The last thing you want to do is create more stress by running late. Lucy Kellaway from the *Financial Times* advises, "Always arrive unfeasibly early. Reduce to zero the risk that speech nerves are compounded by lateness ones." [1]

If you show up at the last minute, you have no time to adjust things. People will be gathering; the minutes will be ticking down. In this situation, there is no way to reorganize and address problems. With time, you can reorganize the room. You can call tech support. You can make alternate plans if you have to.

Several years ago I had the opportunity to present to more than two hundred Northwestern University alumni on the topic of Super Bowl advertising. When I arrived, I quickly realized that the computer sound hookup wasn't working. This meant that I could play commercials, but people couldn't hear them. This was a problem; it is difficult to do a great talk on Super Bowl advertising if people can't hear the commercials.

I realized that I had time; I had arrived forty minutes before the presentation to set up. I also realized that there was a Best Buy just a block away. So I dashed out the door to Best Buy, purchased a set of high-quality Polk speakers and ran back. I set up the speakers and was ready to go. By the time participants arrived, I was casually talking with the event organizers, giving the impression that I was, of course, a supremely well-prepared presenter. Most people didn't notice that I was huffing and puffing, and sweating in my suit.

In most cases, you should arrive at least forty-five minutes before a typical presentation. Your audience probably won't show up until fifteen minutes before the start time. This then gives you thirty minutes to get things organized.

If you are presenting after another person, it is useful to sit through their talk. This will give you a feel for the audience. You can also refer back to their material. If nothing else, you can then be certain that you won't be telling the same joke!

On occasion, you will directly follow another presenter, with no break. This is not ideal; you generally want some time for people to mentally shift from one topic to the next. Still, if the event organizer says there will be no break, you may need to go along with the plan.

In this case, you need to arrive particularly early and set up before the other person starts. You want the transition to be smooth, and the only way to ensure this will be the case is to get there ahead of time.

Check the Equipment

One of the great things about presenting these days is that we have incredible technology. We can project our slides in brilliant color. We can show videos. We can survey our audience using interactive platforms. We can bounce from one slide to the next. It is simply amazing, and in the years to come technology will only push us further forward.

The problem is that all of these technology platforms can go on the blink. Sometimes the projector doesn't work at all. Sometimes it projects, but the proportions are off. Sometimes the sound hookup doesn't operate, and the voting system doesn't connect. Even finding someone to deal with the technical issues can be a challenge. As author Cary Lemkowitz notes, "It is an ironclad rule, even in the most sophisticated companies, that the higher the quality of the audio/visual system, the less likelihood there is that anyone in the room will know how to operate it."[2]

Technical issues are a major problem. They frustrate your audience; nobody likes to sit around while someone sorts out how to work the computer. Time is precious. Technical issues also make you look bad. People don't look their best staring at a projector, desperately hoping it will work, or jiggering cords trying to get devices to connect.

The way to avoid technical issues is simple: check everything ahead of time.

PLAY YOUR VIDEOS

In my experience, videos create more problems than anything else, so these require a special set of checks before your presentation.

Videos are wonderful tools for livening up a presentation. A funny video gets people laughing, and an emotional film can get people feeling sad, hopeful or encouraged.

The problem is that videos can be difficult to use. Sometimes they won't play at all, or they will freeze in the middle, or the sound won't kick in. Sometimes the picture doesn't perfectly align with the sound, a snafu that is surprisingly disturbing.

It is better to skip a video than to use one that might not work; a flawed video playback makes you look unprepared and makes the audience feel bad. They are missing out on what might have been a great clip.

To avoid all these problems, you should test every video before a presentation, playing it several times to be certain that it will work. If there is a problem with a video, you want to know it well ahead of time so you can fix it or cut it.

Videos that require internet access are a particular problem; you may find the internet connection isn't working properly. It is best to download the video file if at all possible. If a video is critical to your presentation, definitely download it. Relying on an internet connection is simply too risky.

TEST THE SOUND

A presentation is all about sound. This is obvious. But it is remarkable how little attention people pay to getting the sound right in a room.

In many situations, a microphone is your best option.

Before starting a presentation, you should spend some time evaluating and adjusting the sound levels. You want the sound to be loud but not too loud, so that it is neither annoying nor distracting. Since a full room will muffle the sound, you should be a little too loud when the room is empty. You don't want to waste time with your audience adjusting your sound.

Asking "Can you hear me back there?" is a tempting way to evaluate sound levels but this isn't ideal. All too often someone struggling to hear will give a thumbs-up. They might be embarrassed to admit they can't make out what you're saying, even though they shouldn't be, and you desperately want them to be honest. Remember that if your audience can't hear you, it is your problem, not their problem. Getting the sound right is critical.

WALK THROUGH THE PRESENTATION

A best practice is to walk through your presentation from start to finish, checking all the different elements. This will highlight any technical issues. You don't need to deliver the presentation at this point; this isn't the time for practice. You just should flip through it.

Show your slides, play your videos, consider what you will be doing at each point. Is the animation in your presentation what you intended? I did a presentation recently that featured a list of ten lessons. I started with number ten and then worked my way down. This went very well, until I got to five. After that things went awry; the number two item popped up next, followed by four, then one, then three. It was a bit awkward.

If you plan on interacting with your audience during the presentation, do you need nametags? If you will be writing ideas on a whiteboard, walk over to the whiteboard. Are there pens? Checking each item will give you confidence and ensure that the presentation will go well.

Arrange the Room

Before a presentation, you should study the room layout and adjust it so that it is optimal for your approach.

There are many ways to organize a room. You can put chairs at round tables or rectangular tables. You can have people sit in a row or in a circle. The room might be classroom style, with people all facing the front, or workshop style, with groups scattered about.

Seating is largely a question of practical logistics. If you have a lot of people, for example, you may need to seat everyone in rows. It is the only way to fit them in. If you have a smaller group, you can spread out and consider different arrangements.

If your presentation will depend on conversation in small groups, then a series of tables might make sense. When you split people up, you can ask them to discuss at their tables. If you don't plan on having small group discussions, then a series of tables might make little sense; it will force some people to rather awkwardly turn their chairs around in order to see you.

LEAVE YOURSELF SPACE

When setting up a room, it is all too easy to forget that you'll need a place to stand.

To deliver a good presentation, you will need to move around. You should wave your arms and stroll the space. This will help make the session interesting and dynamic. You can only move around, however, if you have some room.

If you aren't careful, you will find yourself with tables close to the projector and screen. People who aren't actually presenting tend to set tables in what feels like a logical fashion. They don't have the perspective of the presenter. The room might look like this:

Exhibit 12-1

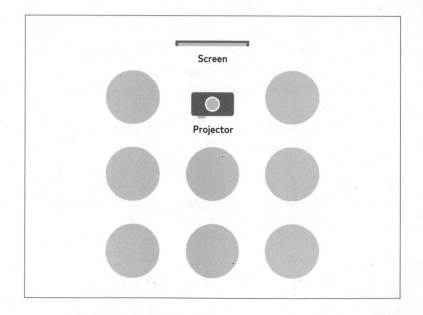

This arrangement is a problem. As the presenter, you are trapped. You can only move about three feet in any direction without bumping into someone. You must stand right next to the screen on one side or the other.

A better arrangement would be to push everything back by several feet, opening up a space at the front of the room for you to work with.

Exhibit 12-2

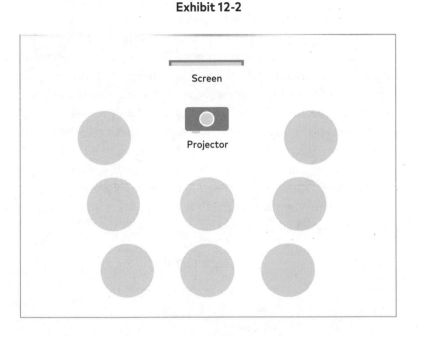

This change opens up space for you to move around. You can move forward and back. You can also move from one side of the room to the other by stepping around the projector. This will look natural and gives you even more space.

One note: moving tables and chairs around is highly disruptive. You don't want to do this once people have started to arrive at a meeting; as soon as people start putting down their bags and materials, you are somewhat locked into a room arrangement. This is yet another reason why getting to the room early is important. You have the opportunity to reorganize things.

WATCH THE PROJECTOR

One of the most important things to watch is the location of the projector.

You never want to block a projector when presenting. The bright light is fine for making rabbit signs, but as a presenter you don't want to find yourself on the receiving end of the bright light. One problem is that the light will temporarily blind you, so you won't be able to see anyone in the room. The other problem is that your presence in front of the light blocks the view for your audience.

Standing in front of the projector is completely wrong. You can almost feel you audience wince when you wander into the light.

So, before the presentation, you should walk the room, checking on the bright light. A good rule of thumb is this: if you can see the bright light shining in your eyes, you are blocking the projector. You want to be cognizant of the light lines, so that you can figure out "safe space" and "troubled space."

Exhibit 12-3

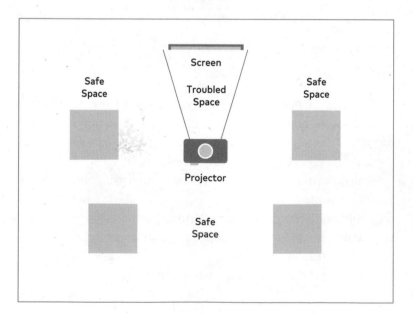

If you will need to move from one side of the screen to the other, you should walk around the projector so you don't block the light. This means you will need space around the projector.

FIND THE FLIP CHARTS

It is almost always a good idea to have easy access to flip charts or a whiteboard. You might not use it but writing on a board is a critical presenting tool; it gives you the chance to explain something in detail.

The key is to have the writing surface ready to go. So, before the presentation, you should check that there are boards in place and available for use, and that the writing instruments work.

Check the markers carefully! You want to be sure you have the appropriate markers: permanent or erasable. If you write on a dry-erase board with a permanent marker, you will ruin the board. This rarely goes over well.

Things can get complicated when you have both a whiteboard and paper flip charts. In this case, you should simply remove all the permanent markers. This means you'll have to write on a flip chart with a dry-erase marker, which isn't ideal. But it can work and it eliminates the chance you'll ruin someone's dry-erase board with a permanent marker. It is very easy to get confused in the middle of a presentation. You have many other things to think about.

Colors also matter; people seem to have trouble seeing things written in green or red; these colors don't pop like blue or black.

GET RID OF THE PODIUM

In some venues, the podium is an imposing structure: large, dark, prominently placed. It is so tempting to use it. You can put your notes right in front of you, along with your computer. You can lean on it. You know where to stand.

Don't.

You are usually better off getting rid of the podium entirely. You should just move it to the side or push it into a closet. However you do it, you should get the podium out of the way.

There are all sorts of problems with a podium. One issue is that it becomes a barrier between you and your audience, which limits interaction and engagement. It is hard to have a deep conversation with someone when there is a podium between you. Your goal as a presenter is to connect with people, to capture their attention and draw them in. The podium doesn't help with this task.

A podium also limits how much you can move. If you are standing behind a podium, you can't walk around. You can't approach people, and you can't move back. You can't naturally walk to a flip chart to write something. You can move your arms only so much; if you lower your arms, they are obscured by the podium.

The biggest issue may be that a podium encourages you to slouch. It is very tempting to lean on the structure. This decreases your energy. It makes you look small and weak.

A large podium might obscure you completely. This is particularly a problem for those of modest stature. The podium's height may block much of your body. You come across as peeking over the top. This does not create an impression of strong leadership. It does not instill confidence. It looks silly. This is why presidential candidates discuss the height of the podiums well in advance of a presidential debate.

Sometimes you can't get rid of the podium. It is simply too heavy, or it is connected to the floor with cords or bolts. In this case, you should either ignore it or use it in a deliberate fashion. You might start behind the podium for your first slide, and then move forward. This gesture signals that you are in command of the space and you are intentional about how you are working the room.

Don't be indecisive about it! Some people move away from the podium, but only a few feet. This looks awkward, a bit like a child learning how to swim; they are comfortable moving away from the wall, but only so much.

POSITION THE COMPUTER

One of the more overlooked tasks when setting a room is deciding where to put your computer.

It is tempting to put the computer in front of you, on a podium or the projector table. This feels natural and safe. It is the logical thing to do.

Unfortunately, this is generally a bad idea. If your computer is in front of you, you will be tempted to look at it during the presentation. It is a screen, after all, and we are all very comfortable looking at screens. We do it all day. The bright light attracts the eye.

Reading from your computer distances you from your audience. You can see your computer; your audience can't. It also limits your movement. It is tempting to stand in front of the computer instead of moving around.

When presenting, it is much better to occasionally look at the screen behind you than to look at your computer. It is a natural gesture. At times when you are talking, you want your audience looking at you. When you are referring to something on the screen, you want them looking at the screen. With gestures, you can control this. You can guide your audience through the presentation:

> Look at me, look at me, look at me... now look at the screen... now back to me... and back to the screen again. Look at that number seven and this remarkable bar chart... and now look at me.

Best case, your computer will be out of sight. It could be on a table off to the side or it might be behind the screen. Either way, you will not be tempted to look at it.

It is good to have it somewhat accessible, in case something goes wrong. I often forget to plug in the power, for example, so the computer will sound its alarm in the middle of the presentation. With the computer relatively accessible, I can easily address the problem.

Remember that you should never be typing on your computer during a presentation. The time to work on a presentation is before the event. Once it starts, your focus should always be on the audience.

Be careful with writing on tablet computers. The concept is great; you can write on your presentation, highlighting certain points. In reality, this doesn't work well; it encourages you to look down and focus on the tablet. This breaks your connection with your audience.

COVER THE CONFIDENCE MONITOR

Presenters love a confidence monitor, a screen positioned in front of them that displays their slides. With one of these, you don't need to look back at the screen when presenting; you can just look at the monitor in front of you as you deliver your talk.

Don't use one.

When you have a confidence monitor, you will naturally tend to look at it. The audience can see this. If the screen is low, which is often the case, you end up looking down. If the screen is high, you look up. This is an issue because you are focused on something your audience can't see. This breaks your connection. It is almost as bad as looking at your computer when presenting. TED's Chris Anderson is quick to criticize presenters who use a confidence monitor. He explains, "Either their eyes are constantly dropping to the stage floor, or they're lifting above the heads of the audience. It can be deadly off-putting."[3]

If you are presenting in a room with a confidence monitor, you should turn it off or, if that isn't possible, cover it with a drape. This will eliminate the temptation to look at it.

FIND A PLACE FOR YOUR NOTES

For most presentations you will have a few notes. You might have an outline of your key points, or a printout of your slides, or just some key figures jotted on a piece of paper. As I discuss in more detail later, an excellent way to appear smart is to be able to rattle off a few precise facts and numbers. It is good to write these down.

As you set the room, you should consider where you will put these notes. You don't want to carry your notes with you. You can't make natural gestures if your hands are full of notecards. Your notes should be accessible and visible so you can easily refer to them in a relaxed fashion; you don't want to go off hunting for your notes in the middle of the presentation.

Don't use the podium! Putting your notes on the podium seems like a logical move, but this will just draw you back to the structure. If you are walking around engaging with your audience, it is then awkward to walk back for a glimpse at your notes. It is sometimes very clear what you are doing. This makes you seem less confident, less in control of the situation.

Think about putting your notes on the first row of tables, on the projector table or on a chair. The precise location depends on the room. Most important, the location should be natural and accessible, so you can walk over to the notes and glance at them in the course of the presentation. You don't want to be seen wandering off. This will just confuse people: Where is she going? Instead, keep the notes close. If you know that your notes are just a couple feet away, you will be confident. If you stumble during the presentation, your notes will be right there, ready to get you back on track.

SET ASIDE SEATS FOR THE OTHER PRESENTERS

Very often you won't be the only presenter; there will be several people participating in the update. You might be going through the overall strategy recommendation, for example, while someone else covers the implementation plan.

It is tempting to have all the presenters stand up front during the presentation. The first person speaks, then the next one steps forward. Business school students love to do this. At Kellogg, many of my MBA student teams like to have the full group stand during the presentation, lined up. By doing this, the thinking goes, the group is demonstrating support and is available to help with questions. I saw a team of students from Cambridge Judge School of Business recently present. They formed a line across the front of the room, each person about four feet from the next.

This is a bad approach. Most important, it is distracting. When someone is presenting, you want the audience looking at them. The focus of the room should be on the person going through the material. You don't want people looking elsewhere. When you have people standing up, you are providing an enticing distraction. People may elect to look at the team. Perhaps John is wearing a particularly snappy suit, Sylvie might be wearing a distinctive watch or Jose just got a poorly considered new haircut.

In addition, people standing up listening to someone else present rarely exude excitement. Why would they? They have probably heard the presentation many times before. There is nothing new here for them. So they will probably look bored. Some might gaze off into the distance, wondering where to go to dinner that evening. Someone might glance at their watch. Worst case, someone might decide to check messages on their phone. This sends the completely wrong message: the presentation is so dull even the team can't focus on it.

The other problem is that people standing around may block a presenter's movement. A room with ample space to move looks very different with four people standing around. The presenter can quickly become trapped.

You can see the problem in Exhibit 12-4. The presenter is completely boxed in. She can't move to her left, because she will walk in front of the projector. She can't walk to her right, because there are people standing there. All she can do is remain in one spot, trapped.

Exhibit 12-4

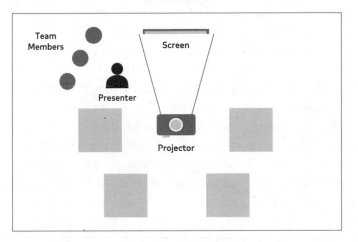

You want to leave the stage to the presenter. This means that you need to identify a place for others to sit. If you have several presenters, you should find a place for them when they are not speaking. A row of chairs off to the side works well; people are out of the way but they can quickly get into position when the time comes, as in Exhibit 12-5.

Exhibit 12-5

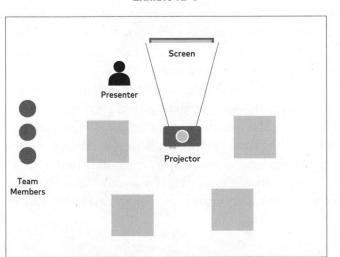

SET THE LIGHTING

Lighting has a huge impact on the overall experience. It sets the mood. Bad lighting can ruin a perfectly good presentation.

In theory, lighting isn't too complicated. You want the room to be dark enough that people can see the slides projected on the screen, but light enough so people can take notes and everyone stays awake.

The challenge is getting this balance right.

The most important thing is to keep the lights up so you can see your audience. Reading the group is critical. If someone has an issue with your presentation, you want to know it quickly. If someone is puzzled, you want to stop and ask if you can clarify something. If the group is bored, you should pick up the pace.

A dark room makes it hard for you to see people; you can't make out their faces. This is a problem because you get no feedback. A dark room may also make people uncomfortable because they can't see their notes.

The worst option is to shut off all the lights. This turns what should be an interactive discussion into something like a Broadway show, when the presenter can't see anyone at all.

On the other hand, you need to make sure the lights aren't so bright that people can't see the slides. This is important with a presentation. It is even more important when using videos. If the room is too bright, people may ask you to dim the lights further. At this point, you may not be able to subtly adjust the lighting, so instead you plunge the room into darkness.

The best case is that you are able to keep the lights up in the room, but dim the lights projecting on the screen.

Be very careful with preset lighting levels! These are often created by lighting people, individuals who are keen on technology, not by people actually presenting. In my experience, preset controls tend to darken the room far too much. This makes it easy to see the screen but difficult for the presenter to see and engage with the participants. Try the preset lighting controls but don't assume they are optimal.

You may need to completely override the preset system. When I present, I usually locate the lighting controls and play with the different options. Can I dim just the light on the chalkboard? Can I turn up the lights in the back?

The ideal lighting may vary during your presentation. Before the meeting starts, for example, you will probably want all the light you can get; so turn on all the lights! More light creates energy. People don't like walking into a dark room; they begin to drift off in short order. Just before you begin, you will want to dim the lights on the screen, shifting to a presentation mode. Then, at the end of the presentation, you bring the lights back up again.

Sorting out the lighting is best done well in advance of the meeting. You don't want people walking in as you are playing with the lights. Turning the lights on and off doesn't create a sense of control. By the time your audience walks into the room, you should know exactly how you will be managing the light levels during the presentation.

FIND THE CLOCK

Timing is a key consideration; you should always respect your audience's schedule. You should start on time and end on time. To do this, you need to see a clock. Best case, there will be a large clock on the back wall, so you can look at it while your audience can't. If there isn't a clock on the wall, you should put a battery-operated clock or your phone on the table in front of you, so you can easily monitor the pacing.

Don't rely on your watch! To look at a watch, you have to turn your wrist and look down. This is an obvious, universal gesture; every time you look at your watch, your audience will know it. They will wonder why you are looking. Are you bored? Looking at your watch as someone asks a question sends a clear signal: their question is not important. They are just wasting your time. You do not want to send this message.

If your watch is your only timekeeping device, take it off and set it on the table in front of you where you can casually glance down at it as you go.

WALK YOUR SPACE

Before a horse-jumping competition, jockeys inspect the course. They come out, dressed in their riding britches, and walk through the series of jumps. They check the turns, look at the barriers and consider the approaches. This is how they prepare for the race; they know what is coming up.

In the same way, it is important to walk your space before a presentation. After you have sorted out the technology, the room layout and the lighting, you should take some time to move around. Walk the space in the front of the room, then walk all around, noting the different views and angles. Remember that all the chairs will soon be occupied. The space between a table and the projector will look very different with someone sitting at the table.

You should consider different questions as you walk the space before a presentation:

- Is there enough room for you to move around?
- How far can you walk in different directions?
- Can you get from one side of the screen to the other?
- Can you get to the flip chart or whiteboard?
- What does it look like for your audience?
- Will the people in the back be able to see?

By walking your space, you learn where you can go. You also become just a bit more comfortable and limit the awkward moments. This all sets you up for success.

13

PRESENT WITH CONFIDENCE

FINALLY, AFTER ALL the development time and effort, it is time to deliver the presentation.

If you've done your homework, the actual presenting should be uneventful. You head into the meeting knowing you have a solid recommendation, people agree with your point of view and your material is polished. The room is set. With all this going for you, things should go well. You are set up for success. Most of the work has already been done.

Still, the actual delivery matters. Things can go off the tracks even at a late moment. Someone might change their view of the recommendation. You may have misread a cross-functional peer and have less support than you thought.

The presentation is a critical moment. If it goes well, you will walk out with an approved recommendation, confidence and a stronger brand. You just have to make that happen.

Nerves

Almost everyone gets at least a little nervous when presenting before a group. It is the rare individual that can walk before an audience without a bit of hesitation or concern.

Even people who present frequently wrestle with nerves. *Financial Times* columnist Lucy Kellaway explains, "Like most people I find public speaking more frightening than spiders or the prospect of being mugged in a dark alley." [1]

Academy Award–winning actress Octavia Spencer shares this fear: "I still have stage fright—anything having to do with live audiences is terrifying. I start sweating profusely, and my heart rate gets really, really elevated. It's the exact same thing every time—the fear never goes away." [2]

Fear is always part of presenting. People in the Confident Presenter segment get nervous, just not as much as other people. Struggling Presenters may find the experience terrifying.

Many students tell me, "I'm just not good in front of a group; I get so nervous." The assumption behind the statement is that people who are good presenters don't get nervous, and people who are poor presenters do. This means that if you feel nervous, you are not a great presenter. Only those who are at peace before a group can claim to be good speakers.

This logic is false. Being nervous, or not nervous, has no impact on your effectiveness as a presenter. I've known people who get exceptionally nervous and present very well. I've also known people who aren't nervous at all, but fail to present well; they sometimes come across as cocky and arrogant.

YOU *SHOULD* BE NERVOUS

Most people are nervous when presenting, and they should be nervous. Getting up in front of a group isn't a peaceful moment. Everyone is looking at you. You have an opportunity to shine or flop. The pressure is on. "Unlike most phobias, being frightened of speaking in public is entirely rational," observes Lucy Kellaway.[3]

Speaker Scott Berkun points out that presenting fear is grounded deep in human nature: "We are programmed to fear standing alone, in open territory with no place to hide, without a weapon, in front of a large crowd of creatures staring at you."[4]

I've been teaching classes at business schools for twenty years. In that time, I figure that I've taught more than 4,000 individual class sessions. That is a lot of time in the classroom. I still get nervous before each class.

So, understand that feeling nervous is natural. Don't expect to present with no fear. You can practice and practice and the feeling won't go away. Ad executive Cary Lemkowitz says telling someone "Don't be nervous!" may be the world's dumbest advice. He writes, "If I tell you not to be nervous, it may drive you right over the edge."[5]

BEING NERVOUS WILL HELP YOU

Fortunately, being nervous can be a positive.

Fear is a good motivator. It can inspire you to spend time crafting a compelling story, proofreading the document and preselling the recommendation. Kellaway explains, "Fear fends off disaster. It discourages you from packing a speech with snarky, teasing asides which, though possibly amusing to you, might be less so to those who are the butt of them."[6]

It also generates energy. When you are nervous, you are on edge. You are alert. You are excited. All of this energy will turn you into a better presenter. You just have to channel it into the presentation. Scott Berkun observes, "If you pretend you have no fears of public speaking, you deny yourself the natural energy your body is giving you."[7]

If you look at stress as a positive, you can completely change your attitude. Being nervous is helpful. Health psychologist Kelly

McGonigal explored this concept in her 2013 TED talk: "When you change your mind about stress, you can change your body's response to stress." When you feel stress, you should think, "This is my body helping me rise to this challenge."[8]

THE CONFIDENCE GAME

While it is almost inevitable that you will be nervous when presenting, you also want to be confident. It is an interesting combination: nervous and confident, at the same time.

Confidence is key to success. If you are presenting and feel like things are going well, you can develop momentum. You relax just a bit. Your mind opens up; you think about the topic and the audience, not yourself.

The alternative can also happen; you get worried and insecure. You think, "Oh, this presentation is not going well" and "I am really bungling the presentation" and "I'm going to forget this key point. I know I will."

When you have the feeling things are not going well, your confidence fades. The nerves kick in and reinforce your insecurity. Your chest tightens. You focus on yourself: your sweat, your hesitant words. You start rushing, then worry that you are rushing, so you slow down, then realize that it all doesn't look natural.

Balancing confidence and nervousness can be powerful. You are on edge, excited, jumpy. At the same time, you are confident that things will go well. I get this feeling each year before the Chicago Triathlon. Before jumping in the water, I feel anxious and concerned. I am confident, however, that I will get through the event; I've done it more than a dozen times, so I know I can get through it.

AN IMPORTANT PERSPECTIVE

One way to boost your confidence is to remember this point: you know more about your topic than your audience.

This is almost always the case. If you are presenting an update on your country's performance to the regional manager, you know more than they do. It makes sense; you spend all your time studying one country, while the regional manager has to deal with several. When you are telling the CEO about recruiting trends on college campuses, you know much more than they do. They might have more experience and a broader perspective, but you know more about the topic. Someone who worked on your business years ago might understand the dynamics, but you know the latest information and trends.

If you remind yourself of this point before your presentation, you put yourself in the right frame of mind. Say to yourself, "Nobody knows more about this topic than I do. I am the world's expert." This isn't just pumping yourself up with empty motivational phrases; it is probably true.

I experienced this dynamic when working on the A.1. Steak Sauce business. A.1. is a very profitable and important brand. Kraft acquired it with the purchase of Nabisco Corporation, and after the transaction closed, I was in charge of the business. I quickly realized that I knew more about A.1. than anyone at Kraft, especially since the prior management team did not stay at the company.

With this insight, I made a series of important recommendations with my team on how to best manage the business. We suggested increasing the media budget, developing a new advertising campaign to reach a new target audience and restaging the struggling marinades line of products.

Each of these recommendations involved a presentation. They all went well, in large part because I was confident about the plan. I knew that I understood the A.1. business better than my manager and his manager. All I had to do was explain my thinking and logic.

FIND YOUR ENERGY

Your own personal energy can have a big impact on the presentation. So you want to put yourself in the right frame of mind. People do this in different ways. An extrovert might gather a group of people to generate excitement. An introvert might take a completely different approach, spending some time alone.

One way to do this is with music. Kellogg professors Derek Rucker and Loran Nordgren recently worked with several other researchers to study the impact of music on emotions. Through a series of interesting studies, the team found that certain types of music generated feelings of empowerment and confidence. Songs with a heavy bass, such as Queen's "We Will Rock You," were particularly effective at making people feel powerful.[9]

Start Strong

The first few minutes of a presentation matter most. You want to get off to a good start. This is true for two very important reasons.

First, with a good start you will have momentum. This will settle your nerves and get you feeling confident. These feelings will propel you forward.

Second, your audience will quickly form an opinion. They will decide if you are credible and if the topic is important. As economist Daniel Kahneman notes, "When the handsome and confident speaker bounds onto the stage . . . you can anticipate that the audience will judge him more favorably than he deserves."[10]

These judgments will form quickly. Penn Jillette, half of the comedy team Penn & Teller, observes, "When you go out on stage, you've got two minutes to get the audience thinking 'This is important' or 'This is grabbing my heart.'"[11]

Jillette is actually being generous with his timing. Studies have shown that people make judgments in just a few seconds (see Chapter 18 for more on how quickly people form opinions).

DRESS THE PART

How you dress has an impact on perceptions. Great presenters know this. Winston Churchill carefully crafted his image through apparel, gestures and symbols. Steve Jobs used attire to define his brand. Personal branding expert Brenda Bence observes, "It's a proven cold, hard reality that people judge you first and foremost based on the way you look, from head to toe. We all do it. It's simply human nature." [12]

Think carefully about what you will be wearing. "Clothes make a statement. The selection of a garment should not be casual or by chance," recommends James Humes, author of *Speak Like Churchill, Stand Like Lincoln*. [13]

When presenting, leave your New England Patriots jersey at home, along with the T-shirt that proclaims, "My parents went to Hawaii for vacation and all I got was this stupid T-shirt." Dress well. Look like you care.

You should be sensitive to the work environment. If you work for a casual company where shorts are the norm and the CEO is likely to show up to the meeting in flip-flops, you shouldn't put on a tie.

In general, you should consider your audience and try to dress a little better. If the senior vice president will be in jeans, you might want to wear dress slacks. If the CEO will be wearing a stylish dress suit, you should put on a suit as well.

STAND UP

You should almost always stand up when presenting. When the presentation starts, get out of your chair, head to the front of the room and begin.

The main reason is that standing gives you control of the scene. If you are standing and everyone else is sitting, then you naturally are the center of attention. People will look at you. You have the power to guide and shape the discussion.

Anyone standing in front of a seated group has a notable amount of power. You can go faster or slower. You can call on people, or not. You can encourage them by looking at them and nodding. You can cut them off by turning away. You can write certain things on the flip chart, or not.

If you are sitting down, you lose much of this influence. People will tend to look at the most senior person, who may then set the pace for the discussion. It becomes much more difficult to cut someone off. How do you stop someone from going on and on with their comments if you are sitting at the other end of the table? You can't.

This isn't the case if the gathering is a team meeting. In that situation, you may well want to remain seated. Your goal is to involve people and promote an idea of team unity and spirit. Sitting draws people out and opens the meeting to discussion.

FIND YOUR SPOT

As you start your presentation, be sure you are standing in the right place. One of the simplest things you can do when presenting is find the right spot.

There are three things to keep in mind. The first thing is that you want to be the center of attention, so you need to find a spot that is prominent. Where will people naturally look? That is where you want to stand.

Second, you want to be diagonal from your key person. There is always a key person, the most important person in the meeting. This is usually the most senior person, but not always; it might be someone who is particularly influential.

If you stand on the same side as the key person, you will block their view of the screen, as in Exhibit 13-1. Don't do this.

Exhibit 13-1

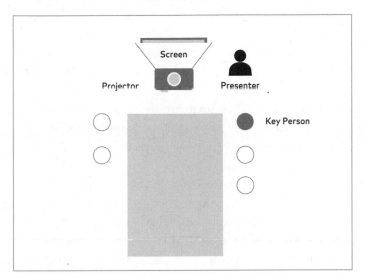

By standing at the diagonal, you give your key person a clear view of the screen and a clear view of you. This will always work better.

Exhibit 13-2

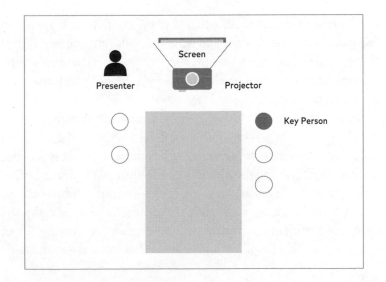

Third, remember not to stand in front of the projector. Anytime you are in front of the projector, you look unpolished. Half the words on the screen are shining on your chest, which makes you look odd and blocks the presentation. You also have a bright light shining in your eyes, which is painful and makes you squint. You are not at your best.

Of course, if you've set up the room properly and walked your space, this all should be easy; you know the right spot to stand and there will be plenty of room to move around.

FOCUS ON THE FIRST PAGES

The first pages will set the tone, so you want to focus on these when you develop the presentation and practice.

There are different ways to start the actual presentation. One approach is to do something crazy and dramatic to get everyone's attention. A different approach is to start with the meeting objective and agenda to get people settled down.

My advice is to get right to the point and start by highlighting the purpose of the meeting. This is not an exciting way to start but it is effective. It is expected. It certainly won't get you into trouble. It is safe.

The dramatic start is difficult and risky. The first problem is that you have to constantly come up with dramatic, unexpected things. In big organizations, people present frequently; there might be several presentations a week. How do you identify all these stunning introductions?

In addition, many meetings have a fairly messy start. Some people will still be talking. Others will be looking at their phones checking emails as you begin. A few people will probably wander in late. It isn't like the theater, where people lock the doors before the show starts. This all makes a dramatic start hard to pull off.

An even bigger issue is that the dramatic start is risky. By nature, a surprising start must always be new, so you are never quite certain how it will go. This means that there is a reasonable chance that your presentation will get off to a rough start. There is nothing worse than a dramatic introduction that falls flat.

So be safe and start with the expected and logical approach. You aren't trying to win the prize for Best Dramatic Performance in a Business Presentation. You are simply trying to get agreement on your pricing recommendation.

Of course, if your audience loves dramatic starts, go with a dramatic start. Ultimately, you are trying to connect with and delight your audience.

Tell the Story

Delivering a presentation is simply telling a story. On each page, you want to stop, explain the main point and then go through the data. You should call attention to the critical pieces of information and explain your analysis.

DON'T READ THE SLIDES!

It is tempting to just read the slides. The words are there, so no thought is required. You can just look at the words and say them. Simple!

Don't do this. Your audience can read; you aren't presenting to small children. As soon as you show a new page, they will get busy reading. If you then read the words that they've already read, they will be bored. You will look stilted and nervous.

Instead of reading the slide, you should just talk about the page. Start with the headline, which presumably has the most important point. You can expand on this in your discussion and move on to the rest of the page.

USE EYE CONTACT

Great presenters look at their audience. Simply looking at someone creates rapport and connection.

This makes perfect sense. If you are telling someone a story, you naturally look at them. It is hard to tell a story to a piece of fruit; you want to see the reaction and watch the engagement. Chris Anderson from TED understands this. He explains, "At TED, our number-one advice to speakers on the day of their talk is to make regular eye contact with members of the audience." [14]

Balance is important. You want to look at someone long enough to establish a connection, but not so long that it seems awkward or makes them uncomfortable. Shana Carroll teaches communication skills at Kellogg. She recommends holding the connection with a single person for a thought or phrase, then moving on to a different person.

TRUST YOUR PRESENTATION

Stick to the presentation! You presumably built a solid, tight deck, so you should trust yourself and your work.

This means that you should talk about each page, in the order presented. When you do this, your audience feels like you are in control. You are sticking with the flow, as you should.

When you deviate from the presentation flow, you send the wrong signal. If you jump from page 5 to page 10, your audience will only think bad things. They might conclude that you didn't create a very strong presentation, so you have to jump around. They could conclude that you are not organized. Who jumps around in a presentation? Most people would agree that would be someone who is a little scattered and disorganized. People who are confident and competent don't do this. If the presentation works better with page 7 presented before page 3, then you should have changed that before you got to the room.

It is particularly important to stick to the flow if you distribute a copy of the slides in advance. If you skip a few pages, your audience may well get lost. Some people will be flipping ahead, trying to find the page you are presenting. Other people will try to read the pages you skipped, in a bid to get all the information possible. Either way, straying from your prepared flow doesn't work well.

Use Precise Facts and Figures

One of your top priorities when presenting is to appear knowledgeable. You want your audience to think that you know the business well. In most cases, you do, so your task really is to ensure that perceptions match reality.

To seem smart, you have to know your facts and figures. Understanding the data is critical.

Now the problem is that there is simply too much data on a business to know it all. There is almost an infinite amount of data. You can't know everything. At the same time, getting your figures wrong can be damaging; it really can hurt your credibility. So what do you do?

There are three easy ways to appear smart and in command of the information. First, you can hedge your statements with general words. This will limit the risk of being wrong. Sometimes you'll get a specific question. Your division general manager might ask, "What percentage of our sales came from Australia last year?" This is a difficult question; there is a right answer and it is easy to check it. How should you respond?

Option one is to say simply, "I don't know. Let me check on that and get back to you." This isn't a terrible answer; it is honest and it addresses the question. The problem is that this doesn't make you seem smart. If you have a good reputation, you will be fine. If you have a troubled reputation, this will be one more reason why you'll eventually be fired.

Another option is to give it your best shot. You step up and confidently say, "Australia made up 8.2 percent of our sales in 2017."

This is terrific but it only works if you are 100 percent confident your number is correct. If you are wrong, if Australia only made up 7.6 percent of sales in 2017, you have a problem. Worst case, someone in the meeting will interrupt and say, "Actually, John, in 2017 Australia was 9.8 percent of our revenue. I have the report here." This is not ideal.

The best option is to hedge your comment. If you say, "I believe it is about 8 percent," you are safe. You aren't committing to accuracy, but you seem well informed.

Second, you can put key pieces of information in your presentation slides. Then when you stand in front of the room, you can quickly glance at the screen, locate the fact and speak it.

You can't put all the data on your slides; this will leave you with cluttered slides that don't work very well. This is never a good idea. But you can put a few figures on the slides. These numbers are there primarily for you to use when presenting or when answering a question. They aren't really there for your audience. "Any visual aids you use aren't just exhibits for the audience, they're giant-sized notes for you," observes Cary Lemkowitz. "You can appear to be speaking extemporaneously by glancing over your shoulder and casually paraphrasing the giant image behind you." [15]

The third way, and in many respects the best way, is to simply write down a few numbers on a piece of paper and leave it on the table in front of you.

You don't want to hold the paper in your hand. This approach can work but it takes away from the effect. You are trying to create the perception that you are an expert, and you are providing the figures just because you know the business so well. It sends quite a signal: "Of course I know the sales growth figure in the Central Region for 2018." If you look at your notes, then it is clear you don't know the figure; you just happen to have notes.

One other tip: write the figure in large print. You want to be able to see the figures from quite a distance. Small type will force you to approach the paper. You might squint a bit. With nice, large numbers, you can easily see them from across the room. In most cases you will already know the figures; the paper is just to give you confidence that you are accurate.

FOR THIS APPROACH to work, you want to identify a few important and precise numbers. You should be completely confident in these figures; you know the source and you should verify the accuracy for each one.

The figures should be relevant and important, but detailed and precise enough that your audience wouldn't expect you to know them with such certainty and detail. You aren't grabbing scattered facts; you are highlighting a few important figures.

Then, as you are presenting, or as you are answering a question, you can just drop in these numbers. If you are answering a question about your proposed price increase, you might mention, "Well, our key competitor took a price increase in 2012 of 3.4 percent, and then took another increase of 4.1 percent in 2017." Or if you are talking about your proposed label update, you might say, "We've changed our label three times in the past thirty years: 1994, 2008 and 2014. The biggest change was that we introduced the color blue in the 2008 update." You are dropping in very precise data in a very casual fashion.

This approach creates the impression that you really know the business. Your audience will probably think, "Wow. This product manager really knows her stuff. That is pretty impressive!" Just be sure the data is completely accurate.

Read the Room

As you get going in your presentation, it is important to read the room and adjust your approach. By looking at your audience, you can predict what they are thinking about and then modify your presentation accordingly.

The easiest signal to identify is impatience. It is fairly easy to tell that someone wants you to move faster. They will get distracted and look at other things. They might flip ahead in the presentation. They take a look at their phone. These are all fairly clear signs.

When you see these signals, you have to pick up the pace. You don't want to start skipping slides; this will create other problems. You can simply present the headline, or perhaps talk about the headline and briefly review the support points, and then move to the next page.

It is also easy to identify when people think you are moving too fast. They might ask you to go back a page in your presentation or to wait before advancing the slides. If you have a printed version of your presentation, they might hang on to the prior page and flip to the next page slowly and with great reluctance.

In this case, you need to slow down. It might be that the material is complicated or you are presenting to someone who likes to absorb the information over time.

Be careful not to inadvertently put down your audience! If you say, "Well, John, I see this information is too complicated for you. Let me slow down a bit," or "Looks like a few of you are having trouble keeping up! Let me go through this one more time," you are making your audience look slow. This will not win their support.

You can also see if people generally agree with your recommendation or if they don't. Agreement cues include a smile, nodding and soft questions. They will look at you with a positive demeanor. People might be leaning forward in an encouraging position or leaning back in a relaxed, positive style.

People who don't agree with the presentation will act in a very different manner. You might get a frown. They might look away. If they are ready to challenge you, actively disagreeing with your points, they will lean in, poised to attack. Often, however, these people lean back. Perhaps they shift from side to side. They might be disengaged or they might be thinking through all the reasons why your analysis is incorrect.

DEALING WITH DISAGREEMENT

If you know that someone in the room disagrees with your recommendation, you should consider taking the time to explore the issue. You are seeking agreement. If you can tell that someone isn't on board, take action promptly. It might be possible to press on and finish the presentation, but it probably won't be successful in the long run. The group might not approve the recommendation. People might share concerns after the meeting, when you aren't even in the room.

When facing disagreement, you might slow down. You could ask if anyone has questions. You might actually call on the person who has the concerns to identify their issues.

You have to use judgment when dealing with objections. Senior people are of course a priority, as well as particularly influential people. Not everyone warrants attention. You shouldn't get bogged down explaining a calculation to a confused summer intern. Your goal is to get enough support to move forward and to identify all the potential issues that might trip up your success.

WATCH THE TIME

It is important to watch the time when you are presenting. Sometimes you will need to speed up and sometimes you can slow down.

Ideally, you want to finish your presentation with some time remaining for people to ask questions and respond to your ideas. So if the meeting ends at 3, you should finish the presenting portion by 2:45 or 2:50.

To make this happen, you need to monitor the time. You should know approximately where you should be as you go through the presentation. If you find yourself tracking behind, you can accelerate a bit. In general, you don't want to skip pages, but you might spend less time on a particular page or exhibit in order to make up time.

Transition Smoothly

It is quite common to have more than one person presenting at a particular meeting, so transitions are important.

You don't want too many people speaking. Every transition is a bit of a bump. It slows down your progress and it forces the audience to adjust. It is often fine to have two presenters in a meeting, or even three. Going much beyond that will often create problems.

Transitions should occur at logical points in a presentation. You shouldn't change presenters in the middle of a section or partway through a story. It just doesn't work very well. For example, don't do this:

> Our pricing issues have been extreme over the past several years. We reduced our prices in 2011. This was a dramatic move but it worked out. In 2014, we started increasing our prices and our competition followed. This was a surprise given that they had lost market share the prior year. And then, in early 2018, we changed our prices again. Now I'm going to turn it over to Susan to continue the presentation.

When transitioning, you should introduce the change and make it as smooth as possible. Explain who is taking over and what they are going to talk about.

Try to avoid changing computers; you should load all the material on one computer. Getting a new computer hooked up is disruptive. At best, the presenter spends time working with the computer instead of engaging with the audience. Frequently, there are technical issues that delay the presentation and create negative perceptions.

It is always a good idea to explain who will be presenting at the start of a meeting. You don't want people to be surprised when you sit down after going through a few pages.

Be sure to wait at the front of the room until the next speaker arrives. It is bad form to leave an empty stage; this will make your audience nervous and uncertain. They might think, "What is going on here, anyway?"

If you are using a wireless clicker with your computer, one nice approach is to hand the device to the next person as part of the transition. This can be an informal, casual gesture, but it sends a clear signal to the audience. You are subtly saying, "I'm stepping aside now and Jennifer has control. You should focus on her."

Close Strong

How you finish a presentation is important; people tend to remember the start and the end. The key is to finish strong, to end seeming confident and in control. A summary page is a nice way to end; it recaps the key points.

At the finish, you need to pause. This is a logical time for your audience to ask questions, so you have to leave time for that. It is also when people will give you their assessment. With any luck, people will approve your recommendation and talk about next steps.

14

MANAGE
QUESTIONS WELL

QUESTIONS ARE A part of almost every business presentation, so you want to think strategically about how you will deal with them.

That is one way a business update is different than a speech or TED talk. In a formal address, there is no place for questions. People don't interrupt the president of the United States during the annual State of the Union address. You don't hear, "Excuse me, I'm confused about the unemployment figure. Is that a year-to-date number or projected full-year number? And what is the change from last year on that?" In a business update, however, there is a good chance you will face a series of questions on a wide range of topics.

How you handle the inevitable questions is important; sometimes, people asking the questions are testing you to see if you really understand the material. If you deal with the questions well, you build confidence and commitment. If you stumble, you can destroy your credibility and weaken the recommendation.

Seek Out Questions

The first thing to remember: questions are good! You want questions.

Questions mean that people are engaged. A lack of questions is often a very bad sign; people might be bored or apathetic. If you are getting questions, you have an audience that is paying attention and interactive. In addition, each question is a chance for you to shine; if you answer a question well, it means that you really understand the situation, which builds your credibility. It is one thing to carefully prepare and deliver a talk. It is another thing to deftly field a variety of questions.

It is easier to respond to questions than to deliver a talk in silence. If you think of a presentation as a conversation, the questions move things along. People can bounce from point to question to point to question. It keeps the presentation interesting and active. Speaking to a silent group is much more difficult.

Managing questions can also be entertaining and fun. It is a bit of a challenge. If you know the topic well, you can smoothly respond to issues as they come up. As Jack Welch notes, "Self-confident people aren't afraid to have their views challenged. They relish the intellectual combat that enriches ideas."[1]

PLAN FOR QUESTIONS

Leave time for questions. If you schedule a meeting for sixty minutes and then create a presentation that fills the sixty minutes, you will almost certainly have a problem. Every question will use time that you don't have. The more questions you get, the more time pressure you will be under.

This can be a problem, especially if some of your key recommendations are found near the end of your presentation. You might never get to the heart of the matter, or you might have to rush your way through it. Neither option is ideal.

You should assume you'll get questions and leave time in the schedule. If you get questions, you will use the time. If you don't get questions, you can end the meeting early. Few people are upset when they get extra time.

SET EXPECTATIONS

People need to know when they should ask questions: During the presentation or at the end? You should tell them this at the start of the meeting.

In general, people will be happy to honor your request. As the presenter, you have certain powers. One of these is to set the expectations. If you say to the group, "I would appreciate it if you would hold your questions until the end," or "Feel free to ask questions as we go along," most people will do that.

A senior executive might interrupt anyway; they are the senior person, after all, so ultimately, they call the shots. If they do, however, then they are making a statement to you and the group.

In general, it is best to have people ask questions during the presentation. Many of the best presentations are discussions, which means you want to have a dialogue. Questions get a conversation going. It is engaging and interesting for you and the audience.

There are several problems with leaving questions for the end. The biggest problem is that at the end of a presentation you want the discussion to focus on the recommendation and, best case, next steps. If you get people debating the best way to move the project forward, you have a successful meeting in the works.

You don't want the conversation to focus on specific questions about the deck. If people start asking things like "Susan, can you go back to page eight? What is the time frame for the first column of numbers?" and "Manu, did you include the fifty-third week in the revenue figures for 2017 that you show on page nineteen?" then the conversation is not going your way. It can be difficult to change course.

Or you might face a tough issue at the very end of the presentation; this is not where you want to encounter problems. If someone is going to say, "You know, John, I think that NPV analysis back on page twelve is way off the mark. Where did you get those figures, again? Can you walk me through the calculations?" you would prefer to get this early in the presentation, not late. At the end, the question sets the wrong tone. Remember the concept of altitude; you want the turbulence to happen when you can deal with it.

If you ask people to wait on questions, there is a good chance they won't ask the questions at all. If someone is confused about a figure on page 4, they probably will not ask about it after you've gone through another thirty pages of material. This is a problem for you, not them. You want people to be convinced. If someone has a question, you want to answer it and address it.

Finally, leaving questions to the end can become a timing problem. How much time should you leave for questions, anyway? Do you leave a lot of time, or do you leave just a few minutes? If your group is highly engaged, with a lot of questions, you might not have time to answer them.

There are only a few times when you will want to avoid the questions. You might have a particularly interactive group. If you know people are going to ask questions and delay the meeting, then you might want to proactively manage the situation so you have some hope of getting through your recommendation.

You might be tight on time. If you need two hours for a presentation, and you only were able to secure a one-hour slot, then you might want to try to push back the questions to give you an opportunity to get through it.

If the recommendation is complex, then you might want to delay the questions, too. There are times when explaining a recommendation requires you to lay out a somewhat complicated story. If this is the case, you might want a clear time to lay out the entire case, assembling each point. Questions might interrupt this process, so delaying them would be best.

MANAGE THE TIME

Sometimes you will need to cut off questions; if you are feel that you are getting bogged down, you might need to stop the flow.

The best way to do this is to offer to answer the questions later. A comment like this works fine: "I would love to take more questions but I am sensitive about the time. I would be happy to answer all your questions after the meeting." You could create a list of outstanding questions. One way to do this is to get a flip chart, write "Parking Lot" at the top and then list outstanding questions as they come up.

Prepare

It is critical to prepare for questions in advance. You should think through the things people are likely to ask about and then consider how you might respond.

PREDICTING QUESTIONS

It is very possible to predict the questions people will ask. This is a useful exercise; if you have a sense of the questions, you can then prepare your answers. If you think someone might ask about 2018 sales figures in the West Region, you can locate this data. If you think someone will ask about a prior new product launch, you can do your homework in advance.

The best way to appear in command of the situation is to nail each question. If you can respond to a question with a clear answer, backed up by specific data, you will come across as credible. When you reply to a question about new products with "Well, we launched the Deliciously Light line of products in 2009, the

Fat Free line in 2013 and the Rancher's Choice Collection in 2016. That was our most recent new product introduction," you come across as an expert on the business.

PLANTING QUESTIONS

Sophisticated presenters sometimes deliberately plant a question to prompt discussion and build credibility. With a planted question, you can prepare a very impressive answer. You can research the key facts beforehand and have them written down in your notes. When the question comes, you just go with your thoughtful response.

There are two ways to do this. One way is to ask a colleague to ask a specific question at a particular moment. You can then respond with a very thorough and polished answer; you knew the question was coming.

A more elegant approach is to deliberately leave a point unresolved, creating an obvious moment for a question. You open the door just a bit, inviting an inquiry. If you say, "This is a bit like Acme's experience in Brazil last year," you are encouraging people to ask, "So what happened to Acme in Brazil?" With the comment "Our competitor learned about social media the hard way," you invite the question "So what happened to our competitor, anyway?"

A planted question is a particular opportunity to shine. You already know the answer. It makes you look in control and wise. If you can take a question and then answer it in a logical fashion, supported by solid data, you come across as a powerful and competent leader.

PREEMPT A QUESTION OR NOT?

When creating a presentation, it is worth considering whether you want to head off a question. If you know there is a point of interest, do you address it or wait for the inquiry?

In general, it is best to proactively address questions. If you think someone will ask about something, just put it in the presentation. Why force the person to ask the question?

To a large degree, anticipating questions is a key approach for writing a presentation. The flow of the document follows a line of thought, based on likely questions. The pages follow a step-by-step flow: the audience will wonder about this, and then that, and then the following point.

Only on rare occasions will you want to leave the obvious question unaddressed. You might want to encourage discussion at a certain point. It might be an easy question that will make you look competent and in control.

What if people don't ask the obvious question? You can still make the point; you just need to pull the question from the air. You could say, "Now, you might be wondering about how our retail partners will respond to this . . ." and then answer the question. Or you might say, "One of the concerns you could have is the issue of timing. Can we execute all this before the holidays?" and then provide the needed answer.

Responding Well

How you respond to questions can have an enormous impact on how people perceive you and your presentation. So you need to respond effectively to each question.

The key, of course, is to know your business well; you understand the dynamics, you know the latest customer research studies and how the business has been performing. With that grounding, questions become a wonderful opportunity to encourage a discussion and get people thinking. The more questions, the better, especially if you've communicated your key points in the executive summary.

LISTEN

The first thing to remember when answering questions: *listen to the question.*

This sounds obvious but it isn't. You will be tempted to cut off the question; you have a good sense of where the questioner is heading, you've thought about the issue and you know how to respond. Your energy is high, you are alert and focused, so you jump in and provide the answer. You think, "You are about to ask about the competitive response! I know all about the competitive response; I've thought about this for hours. Let's go!" Then you interrupt the question and respond.

Don't do this! You don't know exactly where the question is heading until you hear all of it. You also risk offending the questioner. People like to talk and appear smart. This makes them happy, and happy people are more likely to approve your recommendation.

Several years ago, I had the opportunity to participate in improv comedy training with Second City in Chicago. One of the exercises really stuck with me. Each person had to start their sentence with the last word used by the prior speaker. So if one person said, "I think we should get Chinese food for dinner," the next person would have to say, "Dinner..." The exercise forced you to really listen to what the other person was saying; you were waiting and focused on the last word.

The exercise was remarkably difficult; it was so hard to wait and wait until the other person was done. It highlighted how much we like to jump ahead. Waiting for someone to finish is challenging.

BE RESPECTFUL

Instead of cutting off a questioner, you should look at them and nod your head. You should appear deep in thought, intrigued by the question and appreciative of it.

Treating your audience with respect is important. People want to feel that they are valued and intelligent. If you brush off someone's question or demean it in any way, you are sending a signal that you think they are not very important or bright. This is not a productive message.

This isn't always easy. Some people ask ridiculous questions. Other people ask about things you have already covered. Just the other day I had someone ask the exact same question someone else in the room had asked three minutes earlier. They were just not paying attention to the discussion. You will be tempted to scoff at these people, perhaps saying, "Well, John, we just answered that question. Seems like someone is a bit too distracted by their phone!"

This is not a good idea. Remember, you are trying to win over your audience. Don't insult them, demean them or belittle them. If someone repeats a question, answer it in a respectful fashion. Other people in the meeting will understand what you are doing and respect you for it.

REPEAT THE QUESTION

A best practice is to repeat the question, rephrasing it slightly. If the CEO asks, "What is our competitor's pricing strategy?" you might start your answer with "The question is about competitive pricing..."

Playing back the question has three purposes. First, it confirms that you have heard the question and that you understand it. This validates the person asking the question.

Second, it lets other people in the room hear the question. Very often presentations take place in large rooms with difficult acoustics. Someone in the back of the room might not have heard the question. Yelling out "Excuse me, but can you repeat the question?" gets very old.

Third, repeating the question gives you time to formulate your answer. As you rephrase the question, you can be assembling your response. What are the relevant points? What information do I have to draw upon?

You can also subtly rephrase the question, making it easier for you to address it. If the question was "Bob, what was the sales growth in France in December?" you might repeat it as "So, Susan is asking about sales growth in France. The growth rate last year was 3.2 percent." This can work quite well, especially if you know some figures but not others.

You don't want to significantly change the question; you have to remain consistent. You never want your CEO to say, "Ankit, that isn't what I asked. I want to know the sales growth rate in France in December. What was it?" This makes the interaction somewhat antagonistic, the opposite of the feeling you are trying to create.

ANSWER FULLY

The key to answering a question is fairly simple: answer the question as fully as you can. Respond with an answer that addresses the question, providing support points as you go.

If someone asks a two-part question, answer both parts. If someone has a follow-up question, answer it.

INCORPORATE DATA

Your answer will always be stronger if you leverage data. Saying "The cost of production has increased over the past year" isn't particularly helpful or impressive. Saying "The cost of production is up 18.4 percent over the past twelve months" gives a very different impression. You nailed this one.

If you've held back some data points, you can use these to answer the question in an impressive fashion. Ideally, you'll have four or five rock-solid support points held back for use in questions.

The points might not exactly match the question, but that isn't really a problem. Let's say you know, for certain, that average pricing in the category is up by 2.45 percent over the past twelve months. You can use this point when answering many different types of questions.

Question: "Shouldn't we increase our prices next year?"
Answer: "We believe we need to be cautious about increasing our prices; if we raise prices too fast, we could lose significant market share. Across the category, average prices are up just 2.45 percent over the past twelve months. This indicates that there isn't much of an opportunity for price increases."

Question: "Isn't this a risky plan?"
Answer: "There is always risk in a plan, but we think this has a relatively balanced outlook. We are planning on a small price increase. This is consistent with trends in the category. Average prices, for example, are up 2.45 percent in the category. This is very much in line with our proposed move."

Question: "What do we know about our competitor's strategy?"
Answer: "Our competitor appears to be under financial pressure. They are really focused on building profits. Just look at pricing in the category. Over the past twelve months, prices are up, on average, by 2.45 percent. This is just one indicator that profits are a key priority for our competitors."

WATCH

As you answer the question, you should be looking at the person who asked it. This establishes a connection. It is responsive.

Looking at your questioner also gives you a chance to evaluate their reaction to your answer. If they nod and smile, then you know that your answer has addressed their issues. If they frown, however, you know that your answer didn't connect. You might then want to probe, perhaps saying, "Does that make sense, Hugo?" or "Did that answer your question?"

Common Mistakes to Avoid

There are several things to avoid when answering questions. These actions will likely generate a negative reaction from your audience.

LOOKING AWAY

If you look away, you are avoiding the dialogue. If you glance around the room, side to side, perhaps, you look like you are dodging the question. You seem nervous. If you flip through your notes, you may appear desperate, searching in an anxious manner for the answer to this difficult and confounding question.

Turning your back is an even bigger problem. You are not so subtly insulting the person asking the question; you are signaling that the question, and their input, isn't worth your time. This will either diminish the questioner or make them angry.

If someone asks a question, you should respond directly to them. You can look around the room on occasion, to connect with other people, but most of your energy should be directed toward the person who asked the question.

ROLLING YOUR EYES

Any gesture that suggests that the question isn't valuable is a problem. You will annoy your questioner and risk antagonizing the entire group.

You might be tempted to roll your eyes, particularly if the question isn't especially insightful, or if someone is asking their ninth question. Making a snide comment might even get a laugh from the group. But a demeaning response won't help your credibility.

A better response is to nod thoughtfully, respond fully, and then try to not look at the person again during the meeting. This might slow the flow of questions.

SAYING "NOW, THAT IS A GREAT QUESTION!"

Recently I watched a colleague at Kellogg present her latest research on developments in the world of media. It was an interesting talk; she had done some impressive research. This led to a series of questions from the audience.

The first person asked something about measurement. My colleague responded with an enthusiastic "Now, that is a great question!" She then went ahead and answered. She responded in a similar fashion to the next question: "That is such an interesting question." The next person received a chipper "Great question!" and the person after that, "Another great question."

Every question received basically the same enthusiastic response. The only difference was that some questions were "great," others were "super," and a few were "so interesting."

It is tempting to respond to a question in this fashion. It feels like we are praising the question and, in turn, the person who asked it. It also gives us a little time to think about the question and how we should respond to it. We are buying time and warming up the room, all at once. A true win-win situation!

Don't do this.

If you just repeat the phrase over and over, you devalue the meaning. If every question is exceptional, are any really exceptional? Everything can't be exceptional, unless the meeting is in Lake Wobegon, where all the children are above average and all the questions are great.

Using the phrase selectively creates a problem. You have just two options, because you aren't likely to declare a question truly off base. Saying "Now, that is a really dumb question" doesn't win friends with anyone. But if one person gets a "Great question!" and the next person doesn't, you are passing judgment on the quality of questions. People may start to hold back on questions for fear of asking what might be a dumb question, or at least a question that is dumber than one of the "great questions."

The other problem is that the phrase subtly diminishes your presentation. If an issue really is that interesting and exciting, you should have addressed it in the presentation. You aren't playing a game of "Find the Issue." You are fully discussing a topic. That means you should proactively touch on the interesting and complex dynamics involved in it.

As a presenter, your job isn't to judge the quality of the question. You want to engage your audience, answer whatever questions they have and present your argument. Questions are usually good.

Don't praise questions. Just answer them.

Managing Tough Questions

Things get a bit more difficult when you don't know the answer to a question. When the CEO asks, "So, Javier, what is the IRR of this investment, anyway?" and you don't know the answer, the presentation gets interesting. There are several things you can do.

GIVE YOUR BEST ANSWER, WITH CAVEATS

As I noted earlier, caveats give you freedom. If you get the question "What was the sales growth in Poland last year?" you can reply, "I believe it was close to 4.5 percent." This response sounds quite direct but it actually includes two caveats. "I believe" indicates that you don't know—you are giving your understanding, which might or might not be correct. "Close to" allows for some inaccuracy: 4.3 percent is close to 4.5 percent, and 4.8 percent is pretty close to 4.5 percent, too. One could argue that 6 percent is also somewhat close.

This works if you have a general sense for the answer. If you really have no idea, don't guess.

It is good to remember these questions and how you responded. After the meeting you can check the actual numbers and correct yourself if you were off. A simple email will head off many issues. You could write something like this: "Susan, I double-checked the growth rate in Poland and found it was even stronger than I thought. Growth was actually 7.6 percent."

REDIRECT

It is always tempting to redirect the question to someone on your team, saying, "Harit, you've been studying our European business. Do you recall the growth rate in Poland?" This gets you off the hook, transferring the risk.

Be careful about doing this. It may be that your colleague isn't paying attention, isn't ready for the question or doesn't know the answer. In all of these cases, both you and your colleague will look unprepared. Making Harit look clueless takes the pressure off of you, but it doesn't make the overall presentation more compelling.

You should only redirect a question if you are very confident they can handle the question. A best practice is to glance at your colleague before redirecting. If they are alert and attentive, then you can proceed. Best case, they nod, indicating you can direct the question. If they are looking at their phone, staring off into space or just asleep, you should find someone else or deal with the question yourself.

DELAY

If you get a question and you simply don't know the answer, acknowledge this and say you will respond later. There is nothing wrong with this response, particularly if the question is precise and not directly related to your presentation topic. If someone asks, "Who is the CEO of Unilever?" and you don't know, simply say, "That has slipped my mind. I'll check and follow up with you." Just be sure to follow up!

Providing a wrong answer may do more harm than good. If you respond to the Unilever question by saying confidently that Jack

Welch is CEO, you damage your credibility. It will be very clear to people that you don't know the answer. Even worse, it appears that you don't know that you don't know the answer. This is a dangerous combination.

USE YOUR PRESENTATION

Sometimes you can answer a tough question by looking at your presentation, either a slide in the deck or material in the appendix.

I would only do this in rare situations. If the page is coming up in your presentation, you will damage your flow by jumping ahead. You created the presentation to introduce material in a step-by-step fashion. Skipping ahead might damage this flow and hurt the story you are telling. A better response would be "Dan, I'm going to cover that in two pages. Please give me just five minutes!"

If the page is in the appendix, going far ahead will throw you off, too. You will likely look a little disorganized as you quickly click through ten pages to get to the appendix and then go all the way back to the place where you left off.

15

FOLLOW THROUGH

THE CONCLUSION OF a presentation is a terrific moment, espe-cially if it went well. At the end of a long and productive meeting, you will almost certainly be tired, relieved, excited and happy all at the same time. It is tempting to lean back and take a break. It was a good presentation, after all.

Be careful! Follow-through is essential whether the meeting went well or poorly. If the meeting was a success, you want to build on the momentum. If it didn't go well, you need to recover and rebound.

Respond to Questions

The first task after a presentation is to address any lingering ques-tions. Usually there will be a few issues. Perhaps someone asked for a figure you did not have readily at hand or for the chance to review a particular market research study. You might have esti-mated the answer to a question, with a promise to follow up with the actual figure.

Addressing these questions quickly is important; it indicates that you care about the person and the question. Ignoring the question entirely, or responding slowly, sends a very different message. When you are trying to build support, validating people and their concerns is a best practice.

Confirm Decision and Next Steps

Perhaps the worst outcome of a meeting is uncertainty. If people walk out unclear about the resolution, it creates a sense of doubt.

It is all too easy for uncertainty to set in. Someone might have left the meeting early; someone else was responding to emails on their phone. A few people couldn't get there at all. Many meetings take the entire time, so the end is a bit of a rush and a jumble.

So, it is always a good idea to send an email to participants with a recap of the decisions. This will ensure that everyone is on the same page. It also serves as a record. If someone doesn't agree, the email provides an opportunity to voice that concern; you always want to know where people stand.

Reflect

It is useful to reflect after each presentation, to spend some time reviewing what happened. Remember that presenting is an art and you can always be better. Deloitte's Jonathan Copulsky has suggested to me that it is "the speaker's equivalent of watching game tapes."

It is particularly important to do an assessment because presentations are not solitary events. You don't just present and then move on. In most cases, the project continues. There will be many more presentations to come before things wrap up. If you learn from today's presentation, you can make tomorrow's better.

The key is to reflect quickly. Best case, you will set aside some time later the same day to look back at the presentation. If you wait a week, you will have forgotten the details. All too often I let a few days go by, then return to the presentation remembering that there was a wording mistake, but I'm completely unclear about where it was in the presentation.

WHAT WORKED?

Begin with the positives. What went well? It is useful to go through the presentation page by page. At what point were people particularly engaged? Did everyone agree with a specific point? Where did you get questions and respond well?

It is easy to miss the positives; you may not appreciate everything that worked unless you really think it through.

WHAT COULD HAVE BEEN STRONGER?

There are always areas for improvement, even when the meeting was a success. Were there any typos? Often, I find I notice spelling mistakes only while presenting. I look up, see the mistake and wince. Was a particular chart confusing? Where did the flow seem off? When did people have lots of questions?

If the meeting wasn't a success—perhaps the proposal was rejected—it is important to think through the cause.

WERE YOU SURPRISED?

When presenting, surprise is generally not a positive. You want to start the meeting with a good sense for how things will work out. If you have spent time preselling your presentation, you should know generally how people will respond to it.

If you were surprised by what happened during the meeting, it is important to consider why. Were you unable to reach some of the participants ahead of time? Did someone change their opinion? Did a new person show up? If you can figure out why you were surprised, you can take steps to prevent this from happening again with the next update.

The Presenting Cycle

It is useful to think of presenting as continuous cycle, not a one-time event. One meeting leads to the next one as the project moves forward. If things go well, momentum builds for the initiative and for your career.

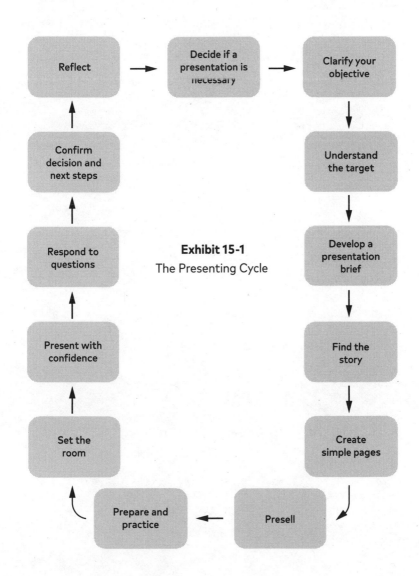

Exhibit 15-1
The Presenting Cycle

16

TED TALKS AND
STEVE JOBS

I RECENTLY ASKED some of my students what they did to improve their presentation skills. One replied quickly, "I watch TED talks! They are terrific."

Another student offered, "I watch presentations by Steve Jobs. He was such a gifted presenter. I try to be like him."

These were not unusual answers. When people think about presenting, they often think about TED and Steve Jobs. These videos are readily available and very impactful.

There is just one problem: they are not particularly helpful models for creating or delivering a good business presentation. Indeed, much of what someone might learn from TED or Jobs simply won't work in a corporate environment.

TED Talks

Consider the format of a TED talk. It is a brief presentation, lasting about twenty minutes. The presenter stands in the center of a big room, often on a carpet or square. The audience is attentive. The room is dark. There is drama. There are no questions, just enthusiastic applause at the end.

This is not how business presentations tend to go. At most companies, people will shuffle in. Some people will be late. Many have coffee, and this will inevitably get spilled. People might have donuts. The conversation is a mix of the mundane ("So, Sally, how did Bobby's soccer game go on Saturday?") and the practical ("John, did you see that email I sent over? I really need you to get back to me on that issue"). There is no spectacle and no drama.

One critical difference: there will be questions. People will ask about assumptions, data and analysis. They will interrupt the presentation: "Hey, Prachin, is that volume figure correct? It looks sort of funny to me," and "What did you assume about shipments in Q3?" and "Did you factor the competitive response into the model?"

Another big difference: people will challenge your data. TED talks don't stress about the source of information. Presenters might say, "There was a study about charitable giving, and it showed that..." They don't cite or show much about the study. Where did the information come from, anyway?

In a business presentation, sources are essential. You can't just say, "I did an analysis, and it showed that Italy is the best investment opportunity..." You have to talk about the analysis. What information did you use? What did you evaluate? Why? This is all critical information to include in a presentation.

Credibility is essential in a business meeting. If you aren't the CEO—and if you are reading this book, then I suspect you aren't—then you probably aren't the most senior person in the discussion. This means that your opinion isn't that important.

The way you get credibility in a business setting is through data. A senior executive might disagree with your opinion. It is difficult for them to disagree with a fact, a piece of data from a trusted source. If I say obesity is a big issue, a senior muckety-muck could disagree. "I think you are exaggerating that, Tim," he might state. "I've seen a lot of surveys and it just isn't as big as people say. Except maybe for me; I've really got to cut back on those sales dinners that David, here, is always taking me on." Everyone laughs and my point is negated.

Data changes the situation. If I say, "According to the US Centers for Disease Control and Prevention, there are 40.2 million obese people in the country. The CDC projects that this will increase at a rate of 3.5 percent annually over the next ten years. Obesity is a large and growing issue," then it is difficult to disagree with the point.

Still, while TED talks aren't a great model, you can learn several things about presenting from them.

TELL STORIES

The most memorable TED talks are built around stories. The presenter talks about a topic, discussing theories and ideas. It all comes to life, however, when the speaker tells a story.

The best stories—the most gripping stories—are personal. It is one thing to talk about other people. For example, the presenter might say, "One day, this particular person did something extraordinary." This can work well, especially if the story is funny or dramatic or surprising. However, when a speaker says, "Let me tell you about the time when I wrestled with severe anxiety," you sit up and take note. They are about to reveal something personal, something intimate, something you wouldn't find on a CV. It is these personal stories that have the biggest impact. These are the moments people remember and hang on to.

You can easily apply this lesson to a business presentation. But there is a limit on stories. Now, in a business presentation, you will need rational strategy and solid facts. These are priorities. You can't just tell one story after the next. The stories have to be sandwiched between content: theories, frameworks and ideas.

SPEAK SLOWLY

The astonishing thing about a good TED talk is the pacing. People speak slowly. They seem to draw out their words. The pauses are frequent and extended.

When presenting, pauses seem unnatural. They are uncomfortable. As a result, people tend to rush through them; we move from page to page and point to point as quickly as we can.

This is a mistake.

Rushing serves no purpose. It is best to slow down, take your time and make your points. Remember that TED talks are highly entertaining even (especially?) when the presenter speaks slowly.

USE DATA

TED talks seem to have the most impact when the presenter uses data to back up their points.

The information varies, of course. Sometimes the presenter talks about a particular study or piece of research. Other times they use stories or anecdotes to back up the point. Either way, however, there is information.

This is a best practice for presenting. If you are trying to make a point, you need data and information to make it all credible.

DON'T USE TOO MUCH DATA

Most TED talks include some data, but not too much. Often, the presenter mentions just one or two studies. This is important to remember as well. You don't want to overwhelm your audience with data, tempting as it might be.

Steve Jobs

When people think of great presenters, they often think of Steve Jobs. The Apple CEO had a remarkable ability to captivate a group of people. He was a gifted leader, a talented product designer and a skilled speaker.

THINGS YOU SHOULD LEARN FROM STEVE JOBS

If you read about how Steve Jobs approached presenting, several important lessons stand out. These are best practices that everyone can embrace and learn from.

Prepare

Steve Jobs was obsessed with preparation. He would show up hours before a presentation to walk through precisely what would happen. He studied the lighting, the setting, the environment. He left nothing to chance.

Many people thought Jobs was somewhat obsessed with presenting. Carmine Gallo, author of *The Presentation Secrets of Steve Jobs*, observes, "Jobs is closely involved in every detail of a presentation: writing descriptive taglines, creating slides, practicing demos, and making sure the light is just right. Jobs takes nothing for granted." [1]

Jobs prepared because he knew that presentation matters and the best way to present successfully is to prepare.

The idea of preparation is one that everyone should embrace. You can't arrive at the last second and do a fabulous presentation. It simply isn't possible.

Keep It Interesting

Jobs balanced showmanship and telling. He had a constant flair for showing things. He wouldn't just say that he had something; he brought it out. He demonstrated it. He let people see it.

This is a key insight into presenting. People love to see things and hold things.

The more that you make your presentations a live, tactile experience, the better they will go.

Limit the Clutter

Jobs believed strongly in limiting distractions. He pruned back each slide to get to the essence. Less is more.

THINGS YOU *SHOULDN'T* LEARN FROM STEVE JOBS

It is tempting to just copy Steve Jobs's approach when it comes time to do a presentation. People think, "Well, Steve Jobs presented this way, so that means it will work for me."

Unfortunately, Jobs's approach is not a model everyone can embrace. There are a number of things Jobs did that people should generally avoid.

Save the News

Steve Jobs had a remarkable way of saving the news. He would tell people about new innovations but he would often hold back a particularly enticing, exciting item. "But wait, there is one more thing," he would say. This would draw people in.

It is tempting to embrace this approach. You put the biggest, most exciting bit of information at the very end. When people think you are wrapping up the meeting, you then delicately say, "Oh, and there is just one more thing."

Don't do it.

Saving the news creates all sorts of problems.

The first issue is that people might not even be there by the end of the meeting. While we would like to imagine that people stay to the very end of our sessions, this just isn't the case. People are busy, often juggling conflicting appointments. As a result, in almost any meeting today, people get up and depart early.

This is a particular problem with senior people, the individuals who will be your critical audience. These people are especially busy and distracted. There is a good chance they will leave the meeting before you finish.

If you save the news, then some people, including perhaps your most important audience, will miss the point entirely.

Remember that anytime you are delivering a presentation you have a task to do. You need to inform, persuade or communicate. If your audience leaves the room before hearing your news, you have failed. You simply didn't get the job done.

The second issue with saving the news is that people won't be able to discuss the matter. If your meeting runs from 9 to 10, and at 9:55 you drop your bombshell news, everyone will soon get up and leave without discussing or reacting to the idea. Again, this is a big problem.

A third issue is that timing might not work out. The most effective business meetings are not presentations; they are discussions. People ask questions, raise issues and debate points. One person in the audience might pose a question of another person: "John, do you think we could really sell that product into Aldi?" This level of engagement is critical. It means that people are paying attention and thinking about the issue.

The problem is that this makes the meeting difficult to manage in terms of timing. You can't really tell a senior person to quiet down. If the CEO has a question, they will ask it. If you are presenting to Richard Branson at Virgin, you can't really say, "Well, that is an interesting question, Richard, but we really don't have time for it right now. Let's try to keep with the schedule, okay?"

A meeting might take much longer than expected so you have to plan for uncertainty.

If you save your news for the dramatic end of the meeting, there is a pretty good chance things just won't work out. You'll be running late so you don't have time. You have to rush the last few slides. Just as everyone is gathering up papers and checking emails, you bring out your big reveal. It simply is not the moment.

Don't Present Data
One of the striking things about a presentation from Steve Jobs is that there often isn't much in the way of data, analysis or calculations. One page might have a single word. Another page could

have a picture. And a third page would have just an image. This created a high-impact presentation, one that was striking in its elegance and simplicity.

My advice is simple: don't do this.

The main reason to avoid this approach is because you are not Steve Jobs and never will be. Jobs could present a word and talk about it, and people would listen and follow it and approve of it. It was astonishing.

The approach won't work for most business presentations.

If you are meeting with the head of a company and produce a slide with just one word on the page, people may well be completely confused. It is a recipe for disaster.

Businesses have hierarchies. Some people are more important and some people are less important. In most cases, the less important people are making recommendations to the more important people.

As a result, a less important person can't just say "Invest" and expect people to fall into line. The senior people will want to hear some rationale.

To make a compelling recommendation for senior people, you need data and information. This requires numbers and facts. You need to show timing, pricing and projected returns. Showing a page with just a word or a picture isn't going to carry the day.

Keep Things Private

One of the truly remarkable things about Steve Jobs was his ability to maintain privacy. He never revealed a product or a project until it was perfect. During the time he was working on it, he ensured that the team preserved absolute privacy.

This worked out well for Jobs, clearly. By keeping things private, he preserved surprise. More important, he protected his lead vs. competition. Jobs knew that other companies would start working on his new products as soon as possible, so privacy was critical.

One might then conclude that you also should preserve privacy and keep things quiet. It would be possible to implement this idea at a company; you minimize updates on your project or initiative as much as you can to protect the surprise.

My advice, again: don't do it.

Communication is essential in a corporate setting. People have to know what is going on. If you keep things quiet, this doesn't happen. Lack of communication creates problems with both senior executives and cross-functional peers.

Senior managers need to know what is happening. You will not do well if you leave them in the dark. If a project is on track, you should let the senior people know. If you make an important decision, you give them an update.

The simplest way to create issues with your boss is to limit the flow of information. You need to communicate more, not less.

The same dynamic works with cross-functional peers. Your colleagues need to know where things stand. If you keep them in the dark, they will probably be frustrated. More important, they won't be able to help.

17

COMMON
QUESTIONS ABOUT
PRESENTING

PEOPLE HAVE A lot of questions when it comes to presenting; there are many issues to deal with. Here are a few of the most common questions I encounter.

Do I have to use PowerPoint?

No. You do not have to use PowerPoint.

PowerPoint is just one software tool that you can use to display information. There are many other tools and these can work just as well, or even better.

When I was a child, I remember watching my father prepare for talks. He was a professor at the State University of New York at Buffalo Medical School. He would spend days working on his presentation and then send the visuals off to a production facility. A week or so later he would get slides back.

He would then start rehearsing. Each slide was about a two-inch-by-two-inch square. To show a page, he would pick up the slide, drop it into his small projector and talk about it. Then he would drop in the next slide and continue along.

My father was quite adept at using his rather cumbersome projecting device. He deftly moved from one slide to the next while he presented. After the meeting he carefully organized and stored the slides; we had a big case in our dining room where he kept all his presentation slides lined up, ready for the next talk.

If you want to be somewhat retro and use this sort of slide device for your presentation, go right ahead. It certainly would make a statement.

If you are an Apple fan and want to use Keynote, Apple's presenting software, do so. If you prefer Prezi, the rather flashy presentation platform, use it. If you can develop your own system, fine.

Just remember two things:

First, only use a program or technique that you are comfortable with. A presentation to the CEO is not the best time to try out a new piece of software. There is a good chance it won't go well, and that will make you look unprepared. It will raise questions and create doubt about your skills and competence. The CEO might think, "If this fellow can't even manage to do the presentation without issues, I can't imagine the project will go well." You don't want this.

Second, remember that the rules of presenting still apply, regardless of the software. You need a title page, an agenda and an executive summary. You should have a headline on each slide. You need support points. Your pages should be simple and easy to follow.

Regardless of the platform, don't just pass out the presentation for people to flip through. You want to use a system that forces you to stand up and take charge of a room. A handout suggests that you can remain seated while you present. This is casual and friendly, but it doesn't help you as a presenter.

When talking to a group, the ability to stand up is critical for attracting and holding attention. The person standing naturally has a prominence in the room. People look at this person. Their voice might be louder and carry farther.

Now, if you are the CEO or president, you don't need to worry about this too much. People will listen to you because they know you have the power to fire them. That is usually enough to hold their attention.

If you aren't the CEO, however, you need everything you can get to take control of the room. People won't naturally defer to your authority and prestige. Standing is one way to get this.

However, you need a reason to stand, which means you need a presentation on a wall. You need something to walk up and talk to and point to. Don't lose your authority by sitting down.

Should headlines always go at the top of the page?

Yes, you should always put the headline at the top of the page.

The reason is simple: people generally read the top of the page first. You want people to get your most important point, so you should put it in the headline.

This approach makes it easy for your readers. They can quickly see the point of the page. If they agree with your main point, they can move on to the next page, skipping over the analysis. Why spend time on data supporting a point you already agree with?

If they disagree with your point, they can look at the supporting information. Just how strong is your rationale, anyway? Where is the flaw in your logic?

Some people recommend putting the key point at the bottom of the page. There is logic behind this approach; the bottom point is a summary of the data above. It only makes sense to reach a conclusion after presenting some data.

In reality, this doesn't work well because you are assuming that people will read the entire page. They probably won't.

Other people like having both a headline at the top and a summary point at the bottom. In theory, this rather complex design brings together the best of both approaches; the headline states the point of the page while the conclusion point at the bottom seals the argument.

Unfortunately, this doesn't work well, either. If you put your main point at the bottom of the page, your audience probably won't ever get to it, in which case you missed an opportunity. If you put your main point in the headline, then the point at the bottom becomes redundant. What is the difference between the headline and the footer? It is all rather confusing.

It is best to keep things simple and put the main point in the headline.

Short presentations are better than long presentations, correct?

No. It is always better to have a simple presentation than a complicated presentation; there are few times when increasing complexity will result in a more effective presentation.

This point doesn't mean that shorter is necessarily better.

Sometimes you need many pages to review a situation and make a recommendation. If you are working on a business that is particularly complicated, you'll need a number of slides to explain what is happening.

Trying to compress information onto a single slide, or just a few slides, can make the presentation much worse. A single slide that presents a complex analysis and the resulting implications probably won't work well; it is simply too much information. You would be better off putting the information on several different pages. The first page might explain the approach, the second page could highlight key assumptions and the third page might show the actual analysis, while the fourth page clarifies the implications.

In many cases, a presentation with eighty pages will be simpler, easier to follow and more convincing than a presentation with twenty pages.

Some of the most elegant presentations I've delivered went on for many pages. My recommendation to restructure pricing for Parkay Margarine, for example, was over seventy pages. I presented a very complex analysis and series of calculations in a step-by-step fashion. Each page was simple and led to the next page. I made a controversial and risky recommendation, but the presentation was so logical that it seemed like an obvious move to the audience.

Should I memorize my talk?

No. You never want to memorize a presentation. Memorizing is bad for three reasons.

First, if you memorize your talk, you will be less convincing. Your goal is to persuade your audience to support your recommendation. To do this, you want to speak naturally and with conviction. You don't want to preach or lecture to someone; you just want to explain your thinking. The best way to do this is to naturally talk about the material, reviewing the logic.

If you memorize a speech, you probably will appear stiff and stilted, with your face scrunched up as you try to remember the next phrase.

This is particularly true if you write out your talk. People don't speak like they write. There is no better way to destroy your image of a confident, savvy and composed presenter than to break into a memorized talk.

Second, it is easy to get flustered when you are reciting a memorized speech. You are so focused on trying to remember things that, when you stumble, it can be hard to recover. It is a bit like the theater on a very bad night. Someone forgets their lines and stands there, helpless. They can't remember the flow; they can't get restarted until someone yells a cue from offstage, perhaps "Steven, how could you deceive me this way?" The actor finally restarts with the help of the prompt.

If you don't try to memorize your talk, you won't forget it. You completely eliminate the risk that you'll lose track of your words.

Remember that in a business talk people won't prompt your next line. Your colleague isn't likely to read off her script: "And that is why we looked at the non-promoted price."

Third, memorizing a talk simply takes too much time. Learning a sixty-minute speech is not an easy task. You have to write out the presentation, study it, memorize it, practice it and then practice it again. If you have a terrific memory, it might go quickly. Most people will struggle. Why devote so much mental energy to memorization? It is better to spend your time checking your logic and analysis.

Can the same document be effective both read and presented?

There is no question that a document meant to be read is different than a document meant to be presented. It is a bit like comparing a book and a film. The story and the material may be the same but the execution is completely different.

For this reason, many people argue that there is no way to create one document that serves both purposes. You can't create one presentation that will be both read and viewed. Jerry Weissman, author of *Presenting to Win*, writes, "A presentation is a presentation and *only* a presentation, and never a document." [1]

The problem is that, in the business world, presentations *have* to play both roles. The same document will be read and presented.

It is important to keep this in mind as you build the document. You need enough explanation and detail that someone can follow it even if they didn't attend the meeting. You also need to keep the presentation uncluttered.

While it's challenging to succeed at this task, a presentation needs to work both ways.

Should I try to be funny?

No. Business matters are not naturally funny. Most people don't break out laughing when they think about a pricing move or a new product introduction. It just isn't an area that lends itself to great hilarity. As a result, humor can feel awkward and forced. So don't do it. As business journalist Geoffrey James recommends, "Leave comedy to the professionals."[2]

Imagine a business presentation where the focus is on humor.

> Good morning. I always like to start a meeting with a joke. Why did the banana cross the road? He wasn't peeling well! I love that one.
>
> Well, now we should get to the new product recommendation. This new product is so good. It reminds me of this joke. What do you get when you cross a bear with a skunk? Winnie the Phew!
>
> Seriously, this is a great new product. We are more excited about this launch than a camel on hump day. A bit like Geico.

It just doesn't create an impression of competence. Instead, your audience starts to think, "Who is this joker, anyway? And why is he working on this project?"

There are three problems with using humor in a business presentation. The first problem is that it sends the wrong signal. If you are telling jokes, it suggests that you don't take the material seriously. That is not going to make your audience feel confident and secure in your recommendation.

Few business topics get better with humor. Does a pricing recommendation improve with a couple good jokes? Will the decision to close a factory get easier with some levity? How about the decision to kill a product?

The second problem is that you can easily offend people in a bid to be funny. This is particularly a concern if you are working in a global business. Humor can be very culturally specific. What is funny in one country can be insulting in another. The risk of committing a faux pas is very high when you are trying to be funny. It just isn't worth it.

The third issue is that the joke might not go over well. If you say, "Let me tell you this great joke," you are setting yourself up for disappointment. What if nobody laughs at all? You then have a problem; instead of building momentum and gaining altitude in your presentation, you have just completely stalled. And for no reason; the joke wasn't essential. It did a lot of damage for no benefit. You don't want to take a risk if there isn't a significant upside.

Now, a certain amount of witty banter is fine. This is particularly the case if you are presenting to someone who appreciates humor that aligns with your style. Nobody likes to sit in a terribly dull meeting. A bit of levity can lighten things up.

If you are going to try humor, I would suggest three things. First, always tell the joke or funny story; don't put it on your slide. This way the moment can quickly fade away if something doesn't go well. Documents and slides can last forever and are easy to take out of context.

Second, be sure you know your audience well. If you don't know the group, then be safe and avoid the witty comment or joke.

Third, make fun of yourself. An entertaining story about your recent travels can work well; you are having fun at your own expense. Just be a little careful. Saying "I am so bad with numbers I'm amazed I remember my ATM code" isn't going to enhance your stature in the organization; it will just raise questions about your skills and competence.

What should I do if I notice a big mistake in my presentation?

There is nothing worse than discovering a significant error in your presentation while you are delivering it. Grammatical mistakes are bad. Mathematical mistakes are even worse.

As much as we try to avoid mistakes, they will happen. How you respond to the situation will have a significant impact on your reputation and career.

Your response should reflect the type of error. If it is a small spelling mistake or formatting glitch, it is best to simply ignore it.

You might just move to the next slide quickly and hope that people didn't notice it. Later, of course, you can fix the mistake so the official file is correct.

A major mistake in the financials is a larger problem.

There are two types of calculation mistakes. One is a mistake in the presentation. Perhaps you flipped two numbers, put a comma in the wrong place or simply inserted the wrong figure. These are notable errors but, as with formatting mistakes, you might be able to move along. If people question the numbers, you can recognize the mistake: "This should actually be 1,792, not 7,192. I will get that fixed. I'm sorry about that error."

A fundamental mistake in the calculations is entirely different. In this case you have to play for time. If the numbers might be wrong, you can't push for agreement; you don't want people signing up for a plan that is based on some incorrect calculations.

At the same time, you can't just end the meeting. If you announce, "Oh, would you just look at that, these numbers are completely off. I wonder how that happened," you will look unprepared and incompetent. This is a career-limiting situation.

The challenge: you need to deliver the presentation while giving yourself the freedom to change the recommendation if the numbers are indeed off. This is not an easy task!

The key is to immediately back off a strong statement; you want to start hedging right away. You could say, "One of the things we've been thinking about is this," and "These are just some initial numbers; we will be getting back to you with a set once we've validated some of the key assumptions." With a bit of hedging, you make it clear that you are planning to have another meeting, at which time you will have updated and more accurate numbers to work with.

How many people should present during a meeting?

You will always be better off with fewer presenters.

It takes a certain amount of time for someone to get settled when presenting. They have to get the feel of the room, adjust their volume and settle into the presenting mode. It also takes time for an audience to get used to a particular presenter.

The altitude principle also plays a role. You always want to spend a bit of time reviewing easy information before you move to more complex and controversial material. Each presenter builds on the material covered earlier in the meeting, to a certain degree, but they have to battle to gain their own altitude.

As a result, you want to have fewer presenters in order to minimize the transitions and disruptions. At all costs, don't have a series of people each presenting for five minutes. This will not go well.

There are times when you will need different people going through the material. Usually this will be driven by endorsement, expertise and politics.

Endorsement is important; there is symbolism in everything. You might start a presentation with a senior executive. This will indicate that the material has their support. By standing up and presenting, they go from being a reviewer or judge to being a supporter, someone who is part of the operation.

Recently I went to my children's school for the annual "Back to School" evening. The presentation started off with the school president welcoming everyone back and wishing them a good year. Then he passed the microphone to the head of the secondary school. The unspoken message was that he fully supported the event but his team was going to cover all the details. This worked well.

Expertise is another reason to shift presenters. There are certain topics that are best addressed by particular people. The sales force incentive plan, for example, will be best covered by someone from the sales organization. The new R&D formulation for a product will be best addressed by someone from R&D; it would be odd to have a finance person presenting the R&D plan. An advanced financial model featuring a multivariate regression should be presented by someone close to the model.

And then there is politics. Sometimes you need a particular person presenting for organizational dynamics. Perhaps they will be offended if you don't invite them to present something. Perhaps your relationship with the finance group is a little rocky, so you need to focus on their support in particular.

Political factors do not necessarily lead to the best ultimate presentation; you may well end up with a presenter who isn't particularly skilled. Still, it is impossible to ignore these dynamics; they matter in every organization. Ignoring politics doesn't mean it goes away. It just means you are more likely to get into trouble.

How can I quickly improve my presentations?

Here are three simple pieces of advice.

First, avoid cluttered slides, especially busy slides that lack a headline. There is nothing worse than a slide full of data.

I watched a presentation just the other day delivered by a senior government official from a major African country. His thirty-minute update included more than forty pages, each one packed with graphs and charts. I tried desperately to read each slide but failed again and again. I didn't have time to get through the page, let alone make sense of it and ask a question.

This sort of update adds little value. It would be far better to skip the slides altogether; all they do is frustrate and distract your audience.

Second, avoid passive writing. You want your writing to be active. There should be a subject and a verb. It should be clear who is doing what. Passive writing, where the subject is buried, falls flat. There is no action.

Consider these two sentences:

- The furry dog bit the mailman.
- The mailman was bitten.

The first sentence works. It is clear what happened and who did it. The dog bit the mailman. The statement moves forward. You might be wondering, "So what happened next?"

The second sentence is flat. There is little action or energy. So the mailman was bitten. I guess that is unfortunate, but these things happen. The big question: Who bit him? Was it the dog? The neighbor? A wolf?

The same dynamic works with business writing. Consider:

* Xenon Corporation launched a major new product this year.
* A major new product was launched this year.

Again, the first sentence has life while the second one doesn't.

Passive writing doesn't just lead to lifeless statements. It also avoids taking responsibility. This suggests that you don't have any ownership of a particular situation. When you say, "I did not ship the product on time," it is clear that it is your fault. You are responsible. Saying "The product was not shipped on time" communicates that someone didn't ship on time. It isn't clear who.

Third, purchase a presenter or, as some people call them, a clicker. You can buy these small devices for $40 or $50. They are simple to use; just plug them into your computer. With a presenter you can advance the slides without touching your computer. This frees you up to wander the room. It also lets you put your computer out of the way. Having your own device is best; it shows people you are prepared and you know how to use it. It is well worth the money.

18

FIVE NOTABLE
STUDIES

THE ACADEMIC WORLD is full of interesting studies that relate to the art of presenting. Here are five worth considering as you develop your skills.

Study 1: The Impact of Big Words

It is widely believed that smart people use big, complex words; bright folks understand these difficult words and use them to communicate with precision. The words also subtly communicate intelligence. Only the sharpest characters use words like "erudite," "fugacious," "promulgate" and "embrocation."

Princeton researcher Daniel Oppenheimer decided to test this belief; he ran five different and interesting experiments and published his results in *Applied Cognitive Psychology*.[1] I'll recap three of them below.

EXPERIMENT 1

In the first study, Oppenheimer selected six personal statements from admission applications to a graduate program in English literature. He then created two new versions. In a "highly complex" version, he replaced every noun, adjective and verb with the longest entry in the Microsoft Word 2000 thesaurus. In a "moderately complex" version, he replaced every third applicable word.

He then showed the statements to seventy-one Stanford University undergraduates and asked them to evaluate the statements for complexity and admission.

The results were quite striking. As predicted, participants noted that the adjusted statements were more complex, with scores for "difficult to read" increasing significantly.

Participants also found the more complex versions less appealing. On a +7 to –7 acceptance scale, participants gave the original statement an average rating of +0.67, the moderately complex version –0.17 and the highly complex version –2.1.

EXPERIMENT 2

In the second experiment, Oppenheimer tested the impact of word selection using two translations of an identical text.

Oppenheimer showed thirty-nine students two different translations of the first paragraph of René Descartes's *Meditation IV*. One version was more complicated than the other, in word choice and grammatical construction. He asked students to rate the intelligence of the author. He told some of the students that the passage was from Descartes.

Students who did not know the author believed the person who wrote the simpler passage was more intelligent. On a seven-point scale, students gave the author of the complex passage a 4.0 and the author of the simple passage a 4.7.

The students who were informed the passage was by Descartes had a similar reaction, rating the author of the complex passage 5.6 on intelligence and the author of the simple passage a 6.5.

EXPERIMENT 3

In the third study, Oppenheimer tested whether making a passage simpler changed perceptions.

He looked at a collection of dissertation abstracts from the Stanford sociology department and identified the ones with the highest proportion of words with nine letters or more. He then prepared a simpler version of each one, replacing every word of nine or more letters with the second-shortest entry from the Microsoft Word 2000 thesaurus.

He showed the different abstracts to students and asked them to evaluate the complexity of the passage and the intelligence of the author.

Participants believed the more complex version was indeed more complex, scoring it 5.6 vs. 4.9 on a seven-point scale.

They also believed the author of the simpler version was more intelligent, with a score of 4.8 vs. 4.26.

IMPLICATIONS

Oppenheimer's studies provide an important lesson. Using more big words does not make you seem smart. Instead, it has the opposite effect; if you use big words, people will think you are less intelligent.

The fact that the findings run counter to common knowledge indicates that they are particularly important to note and remember.

The lesson is clear: keep it simple!

Study 2: Complexity and Choice

One of my favorite studies was done by Sheena Iyengar and Mark Lepper, researchers at Columbia and Stanford. The duo explored the impact of choice on customer preference in a series of experiments.[2]

Here are two of the interesting studies.

EXPERIMENT 1

In the first experiment, Iyengar and Lepper went to the grocery store and sampled jam. One day, they set up a table and opened up six different flavors of jam. Another day, they did the same thing, only this time they opened up twenty-four different flavors: raspberry, strawberry, grape, apricot and more.

They then watched what happened. How many people stopped at the table? What did they do? Did they ultimately buy any jam?

The results were striking. Many more people stopped at the table when there were more jams on offer. With six jams, 40 percent of people stopped. With twenty-four jams, this increased to 60 percent. A big jump!

While the larger selection attracted more people, this interest did not translate into actual purchases. With six jams, 30 percent of the people who stopped ultimately purchased a jam. With twenty-four jams, the figure dropped to just 3 percent. In other words, very few people bought any jam.

EXPERIMENT 2

To further explore the impact of choice, Iyengar and Lepper invited people to participate in a taste test of chocolate. They invited people to sample Godiva chocolate and then asked them to evaluate the taste. As a thank-you gift for participating in the study, they offered people either $5 or a box of chocolate worth $5. This last element was to evaluate purchase interest.

One group of people could choose from six different varieties of Godiva chocolate. Another group could choose from thirty varieties, an entire box of different chocolates: caramel, peanut, light chocolate, dark chocolate, cherry, etc.

The experiment results were interesting, with three notable findings.

People who had more options enjoyed the overall decision-making process more, with a score of 6.02 on a seven-point scale, compared to a score of 4.72 for those with fewer options.

However, people who had more choice didn't like the chocolate as much. They gave it a composite score of 5.46, significantly lower than the people with fewer choices: 6.28.

In terms of purchase, the results were even more decisive. Almost 50 percent of the people faced with the limited assortment of chocolates picked the chocolate as a thank-you gift. The figure fell to just 12 percent for the people given more choice.

IMPLICATIONS

These choice studies by Iyengar and Lepper highlight two important points.

First, people like complexity. In the jam study, people were drawn to the large collection of options. In the chocolate study, people thought having more options was more enjoyable.

Second, having more options makes decisions more difficult. When confronted by complexity and extensive choice, people tend to avoid the decision and are dissatisfied when forced to choose.

In terms of presenting, the implications are important. First, if you ask people what they want, they will tell you they want options, details and complexity. Given the choice, a senior executive will ask for more information and a longer presentation.

Second, in reality, people don't actually want complexity. A dense presentation with lots of details and choices is not likely to lead to agreement and action.

Study 3: Fluency and Motivation

Hyunjin Song and Norbert Schwarz, two researchers from the University of Michigan, studied the impact of perceived effort on behavior change.[3]

EXPERIMENT 1

In the first study, Song and Schwarz gave people instructions for an exercise routine. They first printed the material in a simple font

(Arial, 12 point) and then printed it in a hard-to-read font (Brush, 12 point). The researchers then asked study participants about how long the exercise would take and how willing they would be to do it.

When the instructions were printed in the hard-to-read font, people thought the exercise would take longer and they were less willing to do it. With the simple font, respondents thought the exercise would take 8.23 minutes. This increased to 15.1 minutes when researchers printed the same routine in the complex font.

Willingness to do the exercise fell from 4.5 on a seven-point scale for the simple font to just 2.9 with the more complex printing.

EXPERIMENT 2

Song and Schwartz then gave people a recipe to make a Japanese roll, again printing the same recipe in two different fonts.

The researchers asked people to estimate the time needed to prepare the dish and their willingness to do so. They also asked a detailed question about the recipe to evaluate how much people remembered.

Results were clear. When printed in the more difficult font, respondents thought the recipe would take longer (36.15 minutes vs. 22.71 minutes) and they were less willing to make it (2.85 on seven-point scale vs. 4.21). Respondents also remembered less when the recipe was printed in the hard-to-read font.

IMPLICATIONS

These studies illustrate a simple point. When you make something difficult to read, people believe it will be more complicated and they are less likely to do it. How we present information has a significant impact on how people receive it. People resist things that seem complex.

Study 4: The Impact of Nonsense Math

Kimmo Eriksson, from Sweden's Mälardalen University, did a highly entertaining study on the impact of gibberish calculations on perceptions of quality.[4]

EXPERIMENT

Eriksson selected two published research papers and then created two versions of each paper. The first version was the actual, published paper. In the second version, he inserted an extra sentence, taken from a different paper. This additional sentence included an equation that made no sense in the context of the paper. Here is the sentence:

A mathematical model ($T_{PP} = T_0 - fT_0 d^2 - fT_p d_f$) is developed to describe sequential effects.

He then identified two hundred people who had advanced degrees and were familiar with reviewing research reports. He sent people the different versions of the report and asked for their feedback on the quality of the research.

People believed that the study with the irrelevant math was higher quality.

The impact was particularly significant for people with a background in the humanities, social sciences, medicine and other related fields. Individuals with a math or technical background found the study with irrelevant math to be slightly less convincing. Even among this group, however, adding technical gibberish did little damage.

IMPLICATIONS

Eriksson's study shows the power of complex analyses to strengthen an argument. People, confronted with technical formulas, are inclined to view the research as more rigorous.

For presentations, this research suggests that there is a role for selectively using complex analyses to bolster your credibility. A formula or multivariate regression can increase perceptions of rigor.

Of course, using completely meaningless analyses is not a good idea. It is ethically wrong and someone might challenge the analysis.

Study 5: Quick Judgments

Nalini Ambady and Robert Rosenthal, two Harvard University researchers, did a fascinating analysis looking at quick judgments and behavior.[5]

EXPERIMENT 1

In the first experiment, Ambady and Rosenthal filmed thirteen college teachers and created a video featuring three silent ten-second clips of each instructor.

The researchers then showed the clips to people and asked them to rate the instructor on a series of attributes such as like-ability, professionalism, supportiveness and warmth. From this they developed a composite rating, and then compared this to end-of-semester student evaluations.

In order to eliminate the impact of physical attractiveness, Ambady and Rosenthal had a different group of people score the attractiveness of each instructor.

The researchers also tracked specific behaviors such as laughing, leaning forward and smiling. They then looked at how these interacted with evaluations.

The results were very clear. By looking at three ten-second clips, participants could reliably predict end-of-semester scores, with a correlation of 0.76.

Attractiveness had some impact on the scores, but taking out this dynamic reduced the correlation very slightly, from 0.76 to 0.74.

Behaviors that correlated with higher teacher effectiveness scores included nodding, laughing and smiling, while behaviors linked to lower effectiveness included sitting, fidgeting, frowning and gazing down.

EXPERIMENT 2

In a second experiment, the researchers trimmed the video clips. In one version they reduced the length from ten seconds to five seconds. In another version they brought the length down to just two seconds.

As in the first study, they asked participants to evaluate instructors across multiple dimensions based on the nonverbal cues.

This second study showed that overall scores did not change with the shorter clips, nor did the accuracy of the evaluations. After watching three two-second silent clips of an instructor, people could reliably predict end-of-semester student evaluation scores.

IMPLICATIONS

These studies highlight just how quickly and accurately people form impressions based on nonverbal behavior. In just a few seconds, people can reliably assess a presenter.

This means that you have to focus on your actions, especially early in a presentation. In just the first few seconds, or even before the presentation begins, people are making judgments. Smiling, laughing and nodding—all positive actions—have a large impact.

19

TWENTY-FIVE PRESENTING TIPS

THIS BOOK HAS covered a lot of material, from suggestions to academic studies. Here are twenty-five specific things to remember.

Before You Start

1 Only present if you need to. Do you really have to do that presentation?
2 Clarify your objective before developing an outline or pages.

Creating the Presentation

3 Include the basics in every presentation: title page, objective page, agenda, executive summary and conclusion.

4   Always have a headline on a page.
5   Remember that a headline should be a sentence.
6   Make one point on each page.
7   Connect the headlines. One should lead to the next.
8   Keep charts simple and easy to follow.
9   Don't use many complicated analyses. Be selective.
10 Include credible sources for your information.

Preparing for the Presentation

11 Polish the deck: check spelling, formatting and grammar.
12 Use an easy-to-read font such as Arial.
13 Double-check every number in the presentation.
14 Practice in front of other people.
15 Presell the presentation. Avoid surprises!

Setting the Room

16 Get to the room early to set up.
17 Arrange the room. Think about where people will sit and where you will stand.
18 Hide your computer screen and the confidence monitor.
19 Play music to put you in the right frame of mind.

During the Presentation

20 Look at your audience and tell them a story.
21 Remember that you are the expert; you know more about your topic than your audience does.
22 Trust your presentation. Follow the flow.

23 Explain your analyses and note the data sources. Don't move too fast.

24 Read your audience and adjust: speed up or slow down.

25 Finish early and leave time for questions.

ACKNOWLEDGMENTS

OVER MY CAREER I've had the opportunity to learn from many terrific presenters. It is impossible to name them all.

My first official presentation was that 4-H talk on washing a chicken. My 4-H leaders Walt Hallbauer, Sue Buyer, and Pat and George Jenny got me started on this journey. They were my first coaches and provided encouragement and advice.

At Kraft Foods, I worked with a talented and supportive group. My first boss at Kraft, Sergio Pereira, gave me many opportunities to present and taught me how to do it well. His support launched me on my marketing and teaching career. Susan Lenny held me to high standards. Hugh Roberts tested my strategic thinking, always searching for flaws in the logic. Presenting to Hugh was always an intellectual challenge. Bob Eckert showed me how to be both friendly and commanding in front of a group. It was a pleasure to work with and learn from Rick Lenny, Carl Johnson, Betsy Holden and Mary Kay Haben, four strong leaders with very different styles. Dana Anderson, my agency partner on Miracle Whip, is both brilliant and a stunning presenter.

Since joining Northwestern University's Kellogg School of Management, I have had the chance to watch and learn from remarkable colleagues. Deans Dipak Jain and Sally Blount are model presenters; they command attention and stay on point. Professors David Besanko, Vicki Medvec, Leigh Thompson, Sergio Rebelo, Alice Tybout, Mitchell Petersen, Florian Zettelmeyer, Eric Anderson, Derek Rucker, Greg Carpenter, Lisa Fortini-Campbell and Lakshman Krishnamurthi are just some of the terrific teachers I admire and learn from. Keith Murnighan was a gifted teacher and taught me the power of classroom activities to engage a group and bring a point to life.

A number of people helped make this book a reality. My HBS classmates Brenda Bence and Steven Robbins, and my Kellogg colleagues Alex Chernev, Carter Cast and Andrew Razeghi, gave me terrific advice on the publishing process. Shana Caroll, Eben Gillette, Jonathan Copulsky, John Parker and Craig Wortmann contributed detailed and invaluable input on the book. Jonathan had the idea for the title. I have learned an enormous amount about the creative process from Dan Blank. Julie Hennessy, Eric Leininger, Mike Marasco, Roland Jacobs and Art Middlebrooks, great friends and colleagues, all provided support, encouragement and suggestions.

The production process went smoothly thanks to the help of my editors, Erin Parker and Angela Denk, and the team at Page Two Strategies, especially Trena White and Gabrielle Narsted.

I am particularly thankful to my students. They challenge and inspire me every day in the classroom. Many provided valuable input on this project. More important, they helped me understand the opportunity for a book like this.

Finally, I am thankful to my wife, Carol Saltoun, and my three children—Claire, Charlie and Anna—for making life exciting, rewarding and fun.

NOTES

CHAPTER 1

1   My estimate comes to 5,264 presentations since business school.
    My calculations:
    11 years at Kraft, 2 presentations per week = 1,144
    4 years as an adjunct professor, 2 courses per year, 20 class sessions
    per course = 160
    15 years at Kellogg, 8 courses per year, 20 class sessions per course = 2,400
    15 years at Kellogg, 2 executive classes per week = 1,560

CHAPTER 2

1   Chris Anderson, TED Talks (Boston: Houghton Mifflin Harcourt, 2016), 8.

CHAPTER 3

1   Eric Jackson, "Sun Tzu's 31 Best Pieces of Leadership Advice,"
    Forbes, May 23, 2014 (forbes.com/sites/ericjackson/2014/05/23/
    sun-tzus-33-best-pieces-of-leadership-advice/#6222694d5e5e).

CHAPTER 4

1   Lewis Carroll, *Alice in Wonderland* (USA: Empire Books), 43.
2   Jerry Weissman, *Presenting to Win* (Upper Saddle River, NJ: Prentice
    Hall), 2003, 8.
3   Peggy Noonan, "Make Inaugurals Dignified Again," *Wall Street Journal*, January 5, 2017.

4   Quoted in James Humes, *Speak Like Churchill, Stand Like Lincoln* (Roseville, CA: Prima Publishing, 2002), 27.

CHAPTER 5

1   Quoted in Natalie Canavor, *Business Writing in the Digital Age* (Los Angeles: Sage Publications, 2012), 25.
2   Peter Drucker, "Managing Oneself," *Harvard Business Review*, January 2005, 103.
3   Quoted in Ed Crooks, "GE's Immelt: 'Every Job Looks Easy When You're Not the One Doing It,' " *Financial Times*, June 12, 2017 (ft.com/content/17ee8244-4fb9-11e7-a1f2-db19572361bb).
4   Tony Robbins, "Robbins' Rules: How to Give a Presentation," *Fortune*, November 17, 2014.
5   Quoted in Sam Leith, "Bright Spots, Post-It Notes and the Perfect Speech," *Financial Times*, March 1, 2016.
6   Steven Pinker, *The Sense of Style* (New York: Penguin Books, 2014), 62.

CHAPTER 6

1   Scott Berkun, *Confessions of a Public Speaker* (Cambridge: O'Reilly, 2010), 61.
2   Anderson, *TED Talks*, 33.
3   Pinker, *Sense of Style*, 38.
4   Berkun, *Confessions of a Public Speaker*, 61.

CHAPTER 7

1   Quoted in Nick Werden, "Language: Churchill's Key to Leadership," *Harvard Management Communication Newsletter*, June 2002.
2   Carmine Gallo, *The Presentation Secrets of Steve Jobs* (New York: McGraw Hill, 2010), 1.
3   Daniel Kahneman, *Thinking, Fast and Slow* (New York: Farrar, Straus and Giroux, 2011), 60.
4   Sam Leith, "Churchillian Flourishes That Can Structure a Speech Today," *Financial Times*, November 24, 2015.
5   Anderson, *TED Talks*, 64.

6   Nancy Duarte, "The Secret Structure of Great
    Talks," TEDxEast, November 2011 (ted.com/talks/
    nancy_duarte_the_secret_structure_of_great_talks#t-1075501).

7   Duarte, "Secret Structure of Great Talks."

8   Robert McKee, "Storytelling That Moves People," *Harvard Business
    Review*, June 2003, 52.

9   Quoted in Pinker, *Sense of Style*, 27.

10 Geoffrey James, *Business Without the Bullshit* (New York: Grand Cen-
    tral Publishing, 2014), 151.

11 Cary Lemkowitz, *An Audience of Cowards* (Bloomington, IN: Author
    House, 2005), 94.

12 Gallo, *Presentation Secrets of Steve Jobs*, 13.

13 Pinker, *Sense of Style*, 144.

14 Barbara Minto, *The Pyramid Principle* (London: Prentice Hall,
    2002), 42.

15 Stever Robbins, *Get-It-Done Guy's 9 Steps to Work Less and Do More*
    (New York: St. Martin's Griffin, 2010), 95.

16 Jack Welch, *Jack: Straight from the Gut* (New York: Business Plus,
    2001), 396.

17 Bob Rehak, *96 Proven Principles of Marketing Communications*
    (Kingwood, TX: Rehak Creative Services, 2015), 69.

CHAPTER 8

1   Canavor, *Business Writing in the Digital Age*, 175.

2   Humes, *Speak Like Churchill*, 159.

3   Humes, *Speak Like Churchill*, 160.

4   Sam Leith, "The Pedants Are Wrong—And More Tips for Clear and
    Effective Writing," *Financial Times*, October 16, 2017.

5   Anderson, *TED Talks*, 36.

6   Eli Lilly and Company submission to the US Food and Drug Admin-
    istration, August 10, 2004, 15 (fda.gov/ohrms/dockets/dailys/04/
    aug04/082404/04d-0042-c00034-vol3.pdf).

7   Rehak, *96 Proven Principles*, 69.

8   Gallo, *Presentation Secrets of Steve Jobs*, 88.

9   GE, "GE 2017 Fourth Quarter Performance" (presentation, January 24, 2018) (ge.com/investor-relations/sites/default/files/ge_webcast_presentation_01242018_0.pdf).

10 PepsiCo, "PepsiCo: Frito-Lay North America" (presentation to Consumer Analyst Group of New York, February 21, 2018) (pepsico.com/docs/album/investor/2018_webdeck_final_cagny_gxf9xvfs37bhtpeq.pdf).

11 Gifford Booth, letter to the editor, *Harvard Business Review,* September 2013.

12 James, *Business Without the Bullshit,* 170.

13 Leo Burnett, *100 Leo's: Wit and Wisdom from Leo Burnett* (Lincolnwood, IL: NTC Business Books, 1995), 73.

14 Rehak, *96 Proven Principles,* 132.

15 Gallo, *Presentation Secrets of Steve Jobs,* 84.

16 Leith, "Pedants Are Wrong."

17 Pinker, *Sense of Style,* 9.

18 Pinker, *Sense of Style,* 116 and 121.

CHAPTER 9

1   Ricardo Marques (presentation, Kellogg School of Management, Northwestern University, March 3, 2017).

2   Bernardo Hees (presentation, Kellogg School of Management, Northwestern University, October 10, 2016).

3   Burnett, *Wit and Wisdom,* 50.

4   Anderson, TED *Talks,* 13.

5   Craig Wortmann, *What's Your Story?* (Evanston, IL: Sales Engine, 2012), 58.

6   Wortmann, *What's Your Story?* 39.

7   Kahneman, *Thinking, Fast and Slow,* 63.

8   Hees (presentation).

CHAPTER 11

1   Gallo, *Presentation Secrets of Steve Jobs,* 179.

2   Weissman, *Presenting to Win,* 190.

3   Brenda Bence, *How You Are Like Shampoo* (Las Vegas, NV: Global Insight Communications, 2008), 170.
4   Gallo, *Presentation Secrets of Steve Jobs*, 194.
5   Quoted in HBO video, "Warren Buffett Praises Dale Carnegie Training," February 9, 2017 (youtube.com/watch?v=ucD7fVz7w3k).
6   James M. Kilts, *Doing What Matters* (New York: Crown Business, 2007), 77.

CHAPTER 12

1   Lucy Kellaway, "My Tips for Overcoming a Fear of Public Speaking," *Financial Times*, November 6, 2016.
2   Lemkowitz, *Audience of Cowards*, 65.
3   Anderson, *TED Talks*, 194.

CHAPTER 13

1   Kellaway, "How to Land on Your Feet When Speaking in Public," Listen to Lucy, *Financial Times*, November 28, 2009 (ft.com/content/966d1d74-1d1a-40db-a797-a76076a8ec4f).
2   Quoted in "The Columnists," *WSJ Magazine*, February 26, 2016.
3   Kellaway, "How to Land on Your Feet."
4   Berkun, *Confessions of a Public Speaker*, 14.
5   Lemkowitz, *Audience of Cowards*, 29.
6   Lucy Kellaway, "My Speech Was a Car Crash Because I Am Too Confident," *Financial Times*, April 24, 2017.
7   Berkun, *Confessions of a Public Speaker*, 18.
8   Kelly McGonigal, "How to Make Stress Your Friend," TEDGlobal 2013 (ted.com/talks/kelly_mcgonigal_how_to_make_stress_your_friend#t-723551).
9   Dennis Hsu, Li Huang, Loran Nordgren, Derek Rucker and Adam Galinsky, "The Music of Power: Perceptual and Behavioral Consequences of Powerful Music," *Social Psychological and Personality Science* 6, no. 1 (2015): 75–83.
10 Alison Beard, "Life's Work: An Interview with Penn Jillette," *Harvard Business Review*, October 2016, 128.

11   Kahneman, *Thinking, Fast and Slow*, 4.

12   Bence, *How You Are Like Shampoo*, 187.

13   Humes, *Speak Like Churchill*, 15.

14   Anderson, TED *Talks*, 50.

15   Lemkowitz, *Audience of Cowards*, 51 and 58.

CHAPTER 14

1   Welch, *Jack: Straight from the Gut*, 384.

CHAPTER 16

1   Gallo, *Presentation Secrets of Steve Jobs*, 3.

CHAPTER 17

1   Weissman, *Presenting to Win*, 111.

2   James, *Business Without the Bullshit*, 171.

CHAPTER 18

1   Daniel Oppenheimer, "Consequences of Erudite Vernacular Utilized Irrespective of Necessity: Problems with Using Long Words Needlessly," *Applied Cognitive Psychology* 20 (2005): 139–56.

2   Sheena Iyengar and Mark Lepper, "When Choice Is Demotivating: Can One Desire Too Much of a Good Thing?" *Journal of Personality and Social Psychology* 79, no. 6 (2000): 995–1006.

3   Hyunjin Song and Norbert Schwarz, "If It's Hard to Read, It's Hard to Do," *Psychological Science* 19, no. 10 (2008): 986–88.

4   Kimmo Eriksson, "The Nonsense Math Effect," *Judgement and Decision Making* 7, no. 6 (2012): 746–49.

5   Nalini Ambady and Robert Rosenthal, "Half a Minute: Predicting Teacher Evaluations from Thin Slices of Nonverbal Behavior and Physical Attractiveness," *Journal of Personality and Social Psychology* 64, no. 3 (1993): 431–41.

INDEX

FOR MORE RESOURCES ON
PRESENTING, PLEASE VISIT:

———————————

www.**TimCalkins**.com

www.**HowToWashAChicken**.com

———————————

FOLLOW TIM CALKINS:

🐦 @timothycalkins

in LinkedIn

ABOUT THE AUTHOR

TIM CALKINS is a marketing professor, strategy consultant and author.

He is clinical professor of marketing at Northwestern University's Kellogg School of Management, where he teaches courses that include Marketing Strategy and Biomedical Marketing.

Tim also works with corporations around the world on marketing-related issues through his firm, Class 5 Consulting. Recent clients include PepsiCo, AbbVie, Eli Lilly, Pfizer and Hearst.

His books include *Defending Your Brand: How Smart Companies Use Defensive Strategy to Deal with Competitive Attacks* (Palgrave Macmillan, 2012) and *Breakthrough Marketing Plans* (Palgrave Macmillan, 2008 and 2012).

Tim won the Lawrence G. Lavengood Outstanding Professor of the Year Award, the top teaching award at Kellogg, in 2006 and 2013, making him one of just five people in the award's more-than-forty-year history to have won it twice. *Poets & Quants* included him on its list "Favorite MBA Professors of 2016." He also received the Sidney J. Levy Teaching Award, two Kellogg Faculty Impact Awards and the Kellogg Executive MBA Program's Top Professor Award four times.

He received his BA from Yale and his MBA from Harvard. Tim lives in Chicago with his wife and three children.